Oooo I Say!

Edited by

Chiara Cervasio

First published in Great Britain in 2004 by
POETRY NOW
Remus House,
Coltsfoot Drive,
Peterborough, PE2 9JX
Telephone (01733) 898101
Fax (01733) 313524

SB ISBN 1 84460 781 X

FOREWORD

Although we are a nation of poets we are accused of not reading poetry, or buying poetry books. After many years of listening to the incessant gripes of poetry publishers, I can only assume that the books they publish, in general, are books that most people do not want to read.

Poetry should not be obscure, introverted, and as cryptic as a crossword puzzle: it is the poet's duty to reach out and embrace the world.

The world owes the poet nothing and we should not be expected to dig and delve into a rambling discourse searching for some inner meaning.

The reason we write poetry (and almost all of us do) is because we want to communicate: an ideal; an idea; or a specific feeling.

Poetry is as essential in communication, as a letter; a radio; a telephone, and the main criterion for selecting the poems in this anthology is very simple: they communicate.

CONTENTS

ALL YOU REALLY NEED TO KNOW ABOUT SHAKESPEARE

William Shakespeare, he wrote loads of plays,
He must have been scribbling most of his days.
When geese saw him coming they ran for the hills
Cos he kept nicking their feathers to make new quills.

He married Anne Hathaway, not known to be coy,
And soon had three kids, two girls and a boy.
Born in fifteen sixty-four, when Bess was the queen,
He died on St George's Day in sixteen sixteen.

Will wrote about Hamlet not knowing if he should be or not
And someone called Falstaff, a fat, drunken sot.
He wrote about Kate, a bad-tempered lass
And also of Bottom, a bit of an ass.

There were lots of bold heroes fighting wars to be king
And Troilus and Cressida, who had a bit of a fling,
An old king named Lear, who went slightly mad,
And tragedies a-plenty with endings quite sad.

When Brutus stabbed Caesar the wound wouldn't mend,
Julius said, 'Blimey, Brutus, I thought you were my friend.'
Young Romeo fell for Juliet, heels over head,
They planned to elope but they ended up dead.

But there were comedies too, like Midsummer Night's Dream,
And a Comedy of Errors, with a twin brothers theme.
He wrote of lovers and murderers and men who drank too much beer,
A bit of a lad on the quiet, was our Will Shakespeare.

Ian McCrae

THE CHILD WITHIN

A small boy
Threw his sweets
And stamped his feet
On the floor.
I laughed
Then I realised I did that at work
The day before.

Paulie Pentelow

CAUSING TROUBLE

The doctor pulled, the doctor tugged, the little boy stood watching
And holding tight the torch as no one else was in the offing
The night was dark and he and Mum were left in all alone
It fell to him to manage things and learn to use the phone
He watched the whole proceedings with an admirable calm
Until he saw the baby dangling from the doctor's arm
He watched the smack delivered then across the baby's bum
And saw the pain and agony just suffered by his mum
So when the doctor asked him with a smile upon his face
'How do you like your sister?' it was more than he could take
'I think,' he said quite crossly, 'to be absolutely fair,
You should smack her once again for ever crawling into there.'

Dorothy Blakeman

SO HAVE I!

He left his drink upon the bar,
Went to the loo, it wasn't far.
When he came back his drink was gone,
The empty glass forlornly shone.
He felt upset and quite bereft
For no one would admit the theft.
Annoyed, he bought another drink,
And as he drank, had time to think.
Next time when nature called, he wrote
In large clear letters on a note,
'Don't drink my beer, I've spit in it.'
With hopes it would the thief outwit.
When he returned, his drink was there,
However, what caused him to stare
Hard at his note, what caught his eye,
Someone had written, *'So have I!'*

Jax Burgess

ONE AND A HALF FEET IN THE GRAVE

I sit here and watch, listen in my home
As I cope with all the ailments that come.
That lack of memory, being looked at with pity,
Those pains that descend and almost cripple me.
Still through it all, I must be brave,
Put on a video of 'One Foot In The Grave'
Laugh so much, I just have to pee,
And think to myself, why, that's my husband and me.

Marj Busby

THE HIGHWAY BOARD

The highway board men gathered round,
On each face a sullen frown,
'What can we do to put it right?'
They pondered this till, deep in the night.
Now when I say it was deep in the night,
It was twenty to three and think as they might,
They couldn't fathom what to do,
So one of the bosses said, 'Let's have a brew.'
So off went they to their portable hut,
Quickly inside and the door was shut.
'We can't hurry a task like this,
We have to make sure that nothing's amiss.'
After three cups of the Co-op's best brew,
One of them said that maybe he knew what could be done
                                   to fix the complaint.
He was sent off with the fluorescent paint,
And all down the road strange markings appeared,
I think last night he had too much beer.
Circles here, arrows there,
He sprayed with impunity, he didn't care.
Then along came a wagon laden with tar,
'You can p*** off, it's too late by far.
At this time in the afternoon it's a fight for the door,
Move over, make room,
This task isn't easy, it's a skilled job.'
The boss says this to pep up the mob.
You can't get anyone straight off the dole,
With our expertise to fill a pothole.

Stuart Garrett

—

GET TIDY OF HALLOWE'EN

You've got to tidy your bedroom
before Hallowe'en,
the witches will come
if it's not clean.

When it gets dark
and it's twelve o'clock,
the witches will come out,
let's hope your door's locked.

If your door's open,
in they will come,
sneaking around your room,
better shout for your mum!

But your mum can't hear you,
because the witch has cast a spell,
she's turned into a frog
and your dad has as well.

So you're on your own
and it's the witch against you,
to get rid of her,
what are you going to do?

Grab her broomstick
and whack her on the head,
do it three times
and she'll be dead.

Now you're safe
and your mum's not a frog
and you can sleep
safe and sound like a log.

Stanley Bruce

Afternoon Tea, 1930s Style

'Look at her, at the way she conducts herself,
the lipstick on the cup, and the raised little finger,
just look at her.
She even makes the butler flush and turn away.'
This aside between two nasal, horse-faced women
in the drawing room.
The 'her' in question was
the squire's new wife.
She'd been a chorus girl
and could show them a thing or two!
'Maisie, darling,' cooed the squire,
'Pass the sandwiches to our guests,
that's alright Baines,
you may retire.'
'Very good, Sir.'
Maisie winked at him and tottered up.
It was a fabulous balancing act
That then tilted one woman's hat,
Tossing sandwiches
Into the other's lap.
The red mouth gasped
Blowing kisses
Totally defying the embarrassed faces.

F A C

TRYING TO CONNECT YOU!

You know, I said I'd never get one
But now I've gone and joined the rest
There were oh so many out there
I didn't know what to get for the best.

Three hundred minutes every month
And three months free line rental
Cheap off-peak calls, and hands-free kits
It's enough to drive you mental.

But I think I've got it cracked at last
And with it now, I'm fairly at ease
Though I can't understand, when I ordered a cab,
They delivered fish, chips and peas?

And it sometimes got embarrassing
When trying to act like a figure of note
As I realised that I'd actually been talking
Thirty minutes, on the TV remote!

John Osland

CAT FLAP

Down on Rupert Street lived
the cat lady. Not the bird
lady, that woman lived next door
and they didn't get on. Mrs Curry
took in all the strays over
many days. One day Mrs
Curry in a hurry dropped
her door key crossing the road.
Before she could pick it up
a lorry ran over it. By then
the key was in a very sorry
state. Her one and only key
was now wonky. Mrs Curry
rang me (Luke Warm) a lock-
smith to help her to get back
into the house. Her gratitude
was double payment and my fee plus
a meal, a very good dish.
But I couldn't help notice
how one cat never took its
eyes off me whilst I ate.
Mrs Curry, said, 'Don't
worry Helen, pussycat hates
anybody eating off her plate.'

Vann Scytere

TRAIN JOURNEY

Men on mobiles, women too -
Without this toy what would they do?
Intrusive chat on bus and train -
To me such people are a pain!

Margaret Bailey

T'WATCHER

I am not a twitcher,
Or an ornithologist,
I just feed and watch the birds,
I think you get my gist.

I always spend a fortune
On all the things they need.
Mealworms, feeders
And many types of seed.

I watch them from my window,
It brings me lots of pleasure,
It's just that to continue,
I must find a hidden treasure.

I know they'd like to pay me,
I know my reasoning's sound
From many of their deposits
I keep finding all around.

I'd like to speak their language
But I really don't know how.
Greenfinch, blackbird, robin,
Come on and teach me now.

They do try to communicate.
You think I've gone too far.
Well the proof is there for all to see,
With their messages on my car.

Jean Kelly

ACHILLES HEEL

Addition and subtraction,
Didn't drive me to distraction.

Multiplying and division,
Never led to indecision.

Setbacks with a decimal,
Seemed almost imperceptible.

But four times out of three,
Fractions always baffled me.

Paul Kelly

KNICKERLESS

Who nicked my knickers?
I'm sure I had some on
But when I pulled my skirt up
I found that they had gone.

When I got up this morning
I did as I was told
Mum always said to put them on
Because I'd feel the cold.

I never noticed anything
As I went about the day
I never thought of checking
I'm not made that way.

Whoever nicked my knickers
Put them back where they belong.
It wasn't very nice of you
You know that it was wrong.

I don't know how you did it.
You must have used some tongs.
Just a flipping minute
I forgot, I'm wearing thongs!

Muriel Lobley

MRS FEATHERPOCKET

Mrs Featherpocket put her finger in a socket
and all her hair stood up on end,
she said to her husband, 'May I suggest,
after this, that plug you should mend.'

He said to his wife, 'You live a dangerous life,
you always find trouble, you see,
and when you do something silly like that
you always turn round and blame me.'

Mrs Featherpocket replied, 'What if I'd died,
it'll be too late to fix it all then.'
Her husband then said, 'Why is it so,
These jobs are always left to us men?'

Rachael Ford

THE SLOTH

It was late one sunny morning when Sloth appeared not in a
happy mood
He hadn't eaten very much and was looking for some food
Sloth seemed really desperate as he climbed further up the tree
He soon began to notice there was nothing left to see
All the leaves had vanished while Sloth had been asleep
How could this all have happened? He hadn't heard a peep
Looking very worried now, what else was there to do?
Sloth hung about to think and then went to the loo
He hadn't been for seven days, it was a real relief
It was only when he'd finished, he thought he'd spotted a wreath
The scrummy green foliage looked appetising enough
Only when Sloth started chewing, it appeared to be tough
Sloth chewed and chewed this foliage, but to no avail
Sloth could not understand why he was turning pale
Sloth thought that it was funny but not very plain to see
How something could look so delicious and not stuck on a tree
The wreath that Sloth had chosen had been laid upon a grave
The holly bush had pricked him and Sloth wasn't very brave
Sloth had had enough for now, he sat up and gave a yawn
Sloths are made for sleeping, he thought, and not for getting up at dawn
It was all so confusing for tired Sloth you see
So he slowly climbed back up his precious large old tree
Tired Sloth is sleeping now and he won't hear a thing
Perhaps, Sloth is dreaming about what the next seven days will bring.

Chris Needley

ALL DRESSED UP

There I was, all dressed up - ready to give the speech
of the year to a gathered crowd. As I went to raise
my arm to tell them what I had prepared,
there was a surprise in store.

My belt had broken, leaving my trousers to fall at my feet.
I was exposed for all to see - the scars on my legs
from the passing years.

What should I do? Laugh or cry, or try to hide away
my fallen shame - then I reasoned in my thoughts,
it could happen to anyone on Earth.

Rowland Patrick Scannell

BRIEF ENCOUNTER

Darling it was such a shock
When someone stole your knicker stock
I feel I ought to lend a hand
To cover your dilemma grand
I could adopt a watching brief
And bag that most unfeeling thief
Or else we might go off to bed
Where I could sleep on it instead
As winter draws on chill winds numb
Even the cutest little bum
But Christmas comes but once a year
And Santa Claus will soon be here
For he is Nicholas as well
And what he's bringing few can tell
To cover your needs until the spring
He might bring you a fur G-string
Or has he heard those awful rumours
That you prefer red flannelette bloomers?

Terence Leslie

MEDDLESOME CAT

Peeping round the kitchen door
There's no one about
Looking for something to do
While my master's out.

Running over the dining table
Knocking things to the floor
Leaping to and fro
I bumped into the door!

Climbing on the velvet curtains
Sliding and leaving a few scrapes
Oh dear! I think I'll be skinned
When my master sees the drapes!

Climbing on the window ledge
Feasting on the leafy plant
Doing the business in the dirt
And singing a little chant!

What's that I see over there?
It's a place for me to hide
Help! It's too dark in here
I think I'm stuck inside!

I hear the key turn in the door
My master must be back!
Help! Get me out I screamed,
I'm stuck inside this sack!

I heard my master laughing
When I cried to him, 'Help me!'
I must have looked so silly
When he finally set me free!

Rose Murdoch

NEVER ASK A STRANGER

Lictus went to buy a wife
When slavery was normal
He sought a maid presentable
Correct but not too formal.

He eyed the women up and down
But he was most short-sighted
'I will ask for help,' and on
A passer-by alighted.

'Dear Sir,' he pleaded plaintively
'I've to choose which slave is best.'
He pointed to a tall, slim blonde
'Does this one pass the test?'

'It all depends,' the stranger said
'What your sexual tastes may be
But if I were shelling out the cash
That one would do for me.'

Delighted Lictus left for home
But at bedtime had a fright
When he climbed between the sheets
He'd bought a transvestite!

Sarah Blackmore

OWN UP

Who's just been in to the loo
And had an awful, smelly poo?
They must have left in a big hurry
The toilet stinks and smells of curry.

I'll find out, you wait and see
I'll ask them while we drink our tea
I'll look for someone who goes red
Or looks away and bows their head.

Was it Karl or was it Sue,
I wonder if they did that poo?
Or there again, it could be Bob,
He always does a smelly job.

A woman couldn't smell like that
A man could though, and that's a fact,
'Cause all the food and beer they drink
Would make the toilet really stink.

Upstairs we go to get some sleep
But in the bathroom someone creeps,
We hear a splutter, plop and fart
The toilet's nearly blown apart.

We all peep around the door
And laugh until our ribs are sore,
For out the toilet sneaks my *mum*
And she is almost ninety-one.

Wendy Meeke-Davies

HOME ENTERTAINMENT

I had an aunt
Who lived in Nantes
She played the concertina
With Aunty Flo
On the banjo
You really should have seen her.

And what was worse
Our Uncle Perce
Scraped tunes out on a cello
While Aunt Terese
Did a strip-tease
Whenever she got mellow.

Old Uncle Tom
Read excerpts from
The works of Charlotte Brontë
While cousin Dick
Made us all sick
By doing the full Monty.

Cousin Morgán
Played the orgán
On Saturdays and Sundays
As Grandad Ted
Stood on his head
While wearing Grannie's undies.

Poor cousin Gay
Thought she could play
On Daddy's old harmonium
'Cause brother Fred
One day had said
When she was young she'd play all day
On the linole-ole-ole-ole-ooo-leummmm.

G A Baker

EEC'S TOFFEE APPLE BAN LUNACY

There was a young man from Barnstaple,
Who bought himself a traditional toffee-apple,
But after a few licks
Was surrounded by angry ethnics
And now the young man only eats apple crumble.

R Wiltshire

BODY WORKS

I wish I could get rid of my tum
My legs are alright
They're not such a fright
But
I wish I could get rid of my tum!

I wish exercise wasn't so dumb!
It's so very boring
I'd rather be snoring
But
I wish I could get rid of my tum!

I'm really quite pleased with my bum
It's what they call tight
And I know it's alright
But
I wish I could get rid of my tum!

Of my face I'd rather keep mum
I'd rather not say
How I keep it that way
But
I wish I could get rid of my tum!

My smile is my total sum
I do it a lot
And care not a jot
But
I wish I could get rid of my tum!

So if in your way I should come
Just look at my smile
And don't run a mile
And
Pretend you don't notice my tum!

Sue Percival

PERFECT HARMONY

I was busy with my duster cleaning all around the house
When out the corner of my eye I spied a little mouse.
I gave one almighty screech as I leapt into the air -
Then the little mouse approached me and he offered me a chair!

My eyes were all a-popping and my mouth gasped open wide,
As the little mouse approached me and stood there by my side.
He said, 'I wish you wouldn't scream like that
When I run across the floor
Because when I turned to look around I nearly bashed into the door!'

I nearly toppled sideways when I heard him speak so clear
And I thought, 'Well any minute now he's gonna disappear!'
But the mouse he wasn't budging - he obviously had more to say
And I knew I'd have to listen or he'd never go away!

The mouse said, 'I've been waiting just for you to come along
To see why you are frightened and want to do me wrong.
Why you're setting all those nasty traps to catch me in a snare,
When all I want's a little home so I can settle down somewhere.'

His little eyes were filled with tears and my horror ebbed away
And I felt ashamed inside my heart when he went on to say,
'My wife and children disappeared when
You left the cat in here -
All I've left is a broken heart that's filled with dread and fear!'

I heard myself cry out, 'Please don't . . . don't tell me anymore!'
Then I reached down and I picked him up - right up from the floor.
I stroked his head and I rubbed his fur and he snuggled up to me -
And we soon made friends and live right here - in perfect harmony.

Cora Barras

RIB-TICKLING MOMENTS

Witty moments,
Watching a baby play.
Sportive moments,
Listening to jokes.
Amusing moments,
Dressing up as clowns.
Comical moments,
People falling over.
Droll moments,
As Gran loses her teeth.
Diverting moments,
People laughing at me.
Facetious moments,
Dad dressing as Mum.
Humorous moments,
Baby animals prancing about.
Jocular moments,
Listening to a comedian.
Ludicrous moments,
Watching Dad dance.
Farcical moments,
Grandad falling drunk.
Laughable moments,
Makes life worthwhile.

Catrina Lawrence

THE SUIT

A parcel from Canada, last Christmas,
I opened with mounting joy.
A fleecy suit in a soft green
A perfect fit, *oh boy!*

Invited to London, I wore it,
Walked round the shops with pride,
Stayed for New Year, wore it then too,
And again on the coach for the ride!

As I got home, the phone rang,
My granddaughter's voice I heard,
'Hi Granny, how did you like your *pyjamas*?'
I spluttered and choked at the word!

'Granny has finally gone bananas,
She went all over town wearing pyjamas!'
Oh good grief! That's what they'll say.
I won't live it down for many a day!

Oh well, it's not only the young
Who can wear outrageous attire!
Maybe next year, I'll wear pants on my head,
Then I'll know that it's time to retire!

Honestly though, I thought it a suit!
Warm, cosy, looked good too!
Nobody knows it's pyjamas, so
I still wear it out - wouldn't you?

E M Eagle

IT'S A BUGGER BEING SEVENTY!

The body is on its way out.
My teeth are not my own.
The hair that once was on my head
In nose and ears has grown.

I'm on the list for replacement hips.
You know, the ones that swivel.
My brain switches off like a table lamp
And I end up talking drivel!

Mind you, I've had my moments,
When girls walk past my bench
And the memory starts a-stirring.
Now what was it you did to a wench?

I enjoy my visits to the pub.
A pie and pint are heaven.
I now have time to do what I want.
It's not bad being ten times seven!

Sue Ireland

MY MUM

'Sit up at the table! Eat all your greens!'
Mum shouts at my sisters, thank God it's not beans!
Not the little fat round ones, a thick, red sauce.
Not again on the telly - Inspector Morse.

'Tidy your room, look at this mess,'
Mum shouts at my sisters, who mumble a 'yes'.
Clothes on the floor, books on the bed,
Mum's looking quite cross, her face is quite red.

'Plates in the dishwasher, clear that table,'
Mum shouts after meals, she knows that we're able.
It's raining outside, the cat's at the door,
Mum'll shout again soon, he's muddied the floor.

'Get up for school, have you got your lunch?'
Mum shouts in the mornings, she's got a hunch
That we do this deliberately and cause all this bother,
And we do it because we definitely love her!

Siân Mernor

PETER P EWING

What are you doing, Peter P Ewing?
'I'm stewing,' said Peter P Ewing.
What are you stewing, Peter P Ewing?
'Socks that are pewing,'
Said Peter P Ewing.

What are you doing, Peter P Ewing?
'I'm brewing,' said Peter P Ewing.
What are you brewing, Peter P Ewing?
'Tea from the water
of the socks that were stewing,'
Said Peter P Ewing.

What are you doing, Peter P Ewing?
'I'm chewing,' said Peter P Ewing.
What are you chewing, Peter P Ewing?
'Lumps from the tea that was brewing,
from the water of the socks that were stewing,'
Said Peter P Ewing.

Sue Tobin

A NUTTY RHYME

Our neighbour was out, grass to cut,
His mower was going fut, fut.
He feeds all the birds,
Surprised by his worlds,
'A squirrel has nibbled my nuts.'

Betty Hattersley

ODE TO THE UK CAFÉ

You can keep all your Spanish olé,
Give me a good seaside café.
If the sign says, 'Greasy Egg And Spoon',
Guaranteed, I'll start whistling soon.

Add ten calories when you're breathing in,
Stay a big longer to oil your dry skin.
The most dubious food that's under the sun,
Layered on toast, or wedged in a bun.

Add vinegar, salt, pepper and sauce,
'Change from a fiver? Yes Sir, of course!
Just wait while I pour you a large mug of tea,
If it came any darker, we'd give it for free!'

So here I sit with my working man's platter,
Oh look it's raining, oh well, no matter!
Double my order and pass me the paper,
I'll worry about my diet plan later!

Eric Ferris

HOUSEWORK

I hate that droning *'vroom'* sound
the monster makes as it zooms around
my feet.
And I try to run
but it thinks it's fun
to make my mess look neat!

I pull my stuff
out of its path
but it can simply go too fast
and before I know it, it's all gone,
into the tube and the great beyond.

Whilst it's the truth - I'd never lie -
I'll think they'll find it hard to try
and believe the story I must tell -
My homework was got by the Hoover from Hell - !

Amy McLaughlan

UNFORTUNATE FACE

My mother whilst out in the car with me
Poised with her elegant grace
Said, all of a sudden, as she espied a girl,
'What a very unfortunate face!'

From her toes to her fingertips she's so full of grace,
It's the front that has the unfortunate face!

My mother, it seems, has an eye for these things
Not in a political race
Everything's there, the girl even has flair,
Just an unfortunate face!

From her toes to her fingertips she's so full of grace,
It's the front that has the unfortunate face!

Two eyes and a nose (which turns up at the tip)
Lips like a thin pencil line
Her ears are lopsided - her chin has a dip
But bless her, she thinks she's divine.

From her toes to her fingertips she's so full of grace,
It's the front that has the unfortunate face!

You know there's a saying - quite a popular one
It says, 'Ignorance is such bliss'
The proof's in the pudding, some people would say,
The deluded girl thinks she's a dish!

From her toes to her fingertips she's so full of grace,
It's the front that has the unfortunate face!

Beauty's not skin deep, it comes from within
She's honest, has charm and a quick wit
She's clever and diligent, but still on her own
Though with animals she's such a big hit - poor git!

From her toes to her fingertips she's so full of grace,
It's the front that has the unfortunate face!

So, next time you're out and about with a friend
Just remember, my mum's on the case
Is it you she has spotted whilst walking along,
Is *yours* the unfortunate face?

From her toes to her fingertips she's so full of grace,
It's the front that has the unfortunate face!

Sue Elle

BUSY STREET

I walk, as I do most days of the week,
Up the same street

And the same lady carries too much shopping
And wobbles like an overbalanced vessel.

She is looking at me and thinking,
What *is* she wearing?

And I am looking at her and thinking
What *has* she bought?

It is mostly a day when all I want is to be outside,
Not in her shopping, stuck like a bird in a plastic ring.

She is looking at me and thinking,
She should do *something* with that hair!

And I am looking at her and thinking
She should do *something* about those leggings!

And we both laugh at each other
And are quite content.

Wendy Jane Blair

NOCTURNAL ACTIVITIES

It happened one rainy night,
She awoke with an eerie fright.
She was sure she could hear a 'ribbit'
Although she wasn't really with it.

Downstairs she did trot
To see what the cats had got,
But nothing she could find,
Oh! It was a bind.

Back in bed, no sleep she found,
And still she could hear that sound.
She crept quietly down the stair,
To find a frog was sitting there.

Grabbing it she unlocked the door,
As the rain it continued to pour.
At the pond she released the beast,
On which the cats had tried to feast.

Standing there in the moonlight,
She had another terrible fright.
A shiver went from head to toes,
She wasn't wearing any clothes!

Libi Garner

WHEN I DYE MY HAIR ORANGE

When I'm a very old lady
I won't care what people say,
I'll dye my hair bright orange,
Jog to the shops every day.

I'll wear a gaudy coat
And shoes of purple and black,
If by any chance it's raining,
I'll don my mint green mac.

Though I may seem a bit nutty,
I can face the world with a chuckle;
While others are following fashion,
I adorn all my clothes with a buckle.

I'll join a group of protestors,
All marching for animal rights,
Protecting the Earth to the last,
A union of elderly knights.

If shopkeepers wish to patronise,
By calling me 'darling' and 'dear',
I'll tell them to 'stick' their goods
And go to the pub for a beer.

I know married men will love me,
For I'm always game for a laugh.
If any of them come on too strong,
I'll tell them I'll blow the gaff!

If the family try to disown me,
Thinking I'm rather strange,
I'll do something more to shock them -
I'll join the rifle range.

They may chastise me for drinking
And begrudge me my bottles of gin,
But I'll get extremely angry
If they throw them all in the bin.

So when my life is over,
The best times will really begin,
For when they read my new will
And see they get only the gin!

Marian Jones

RELAXING

I'd taken a week's holiday to stay home and relax -
To do a little housework - forget PC and fax.
I started doing the dishes, to find two glasses stuck,
I tried to prise them both apart and broke them - just my luck!
I did some of the ironing (everyone's but my own)
Mine would have to wait a while - the plug had gone and blown.
I thought I'd do the cleaning, the floor was hoarding fluff.
I moved the hoover back and forth and thought it really tough.
I realised it wasn't working - not sucking up at all,
Instead of picking up the dirt it blew it up the hall.
I tried to fix the dust bag, but found it was all torn,
And when I finally changed it - found the motor worn.
I made myself a cup of tea and sat down for a rest,
But a sudden thud from the fireplace revealed a fallen nest.
The soot came down in sackfuls and settled inches thick,
Of course my tea went flying as I jumped up far too quick.
My clothes went in the washer - all filthy, black and soiled,
And came out just as dirty, although they had been boiled.
The thermostat was broken so I phoned up 'Washa Fix'
They said it was too late to call - they always closed at six.
Good grief! Where had the time gone? I looked and felt a sight -
My husband and the children would get an awful fright!
'That's it!' I screamed. 'I've had enough, we'll just go out for tea.'
Tomorrow I'll go back to work - relaxing's not for me!

Marian Williams

INFERNAL MACHINE

What is this thing?
That can't get worse
It devours water
With and endless thirst.

It goes through the day
With rattles and moans
Then when nears the end
Lets out one endless groan.

Then it all starts again
With a whine and a grate
Maybe something inside
That's become quite a state.

A bush or bearing
In need of repair
This infernal machine
Gives me fits of despair.

Guess I'll just have to get a new washer.

Leslie Tomlinson

Is This Love?

I saw a true wondrous beauty,
As I was slowly walking by,
So I walked by once more gain,
I just had to do this duty.
She smiled a little smile
And my face began to glow,
She fluttered her eyes before me,
My heart was surely struck so.
Walking by for a third time,
She arose and came to me.
Radiant, wonderful, awesome,
An angel, so shining was she.
My mouth was unable to speak,
My heart was all of a flutter,
Knees were trembling, feeling weak,
I just could not find words to utter.
But then my face began to frown,
For slowly she passed me right by,
My heart sank low, way back down,
She walked into the arms of her guy!

C R Slater

SUCH IS LIFE

I have got a teenage daughter
yes, I knew you'd sympathise,
I can tell you have one also,
by that crazed look in your eyes.
Her life is one long crisis,
all her friends are just as mad,
I should be mentioned in dispatches
for the aggro that I've had!
The house is full of girlish screams,
make-up and loud CDs,
I swear their only motive
is to bring me to my knees!
They're full of machinations,
(that's cunning plots and ploys)
on how to go about their aim
of reeling in the boys.
My hair's like unfinished knitting,
my cool I can't sustain,
the artful little minxes
are driving me insane.
But when I cast my mind back
I think 'twas ever thus,
for my mother used to say to me
you girls are not like us!
So I'll smile at my long-suffering husband
who worships the quicksand I walk on
and we'll lock ourselves up in the bedroom
to re-kindle our long standing option!

Margaret A Mattinson

DINNER LADIES

It's midday and the buzzer sounds -
Ladies patrol the school and grounds.
There's chaos and mayhem in the hall,
As a pupil trips - lunch up the wall!
Mop and bucket, out it comes,
Washing away the mess and crumbs.
Pupils in - then out they go
Some dither, they aren't half slow!
A food fight erupts behind my back,
Undoubtedly it's Joe or Jack.
A UFO flies across the room,
Still an hour left - it's only noon!
Hot and bothered I patrol outside,
In time to see two boys collide,
With two bumped heads and bloodstained knees
Will some one else take over - *please!*
So as Margaret goes in the Medical Room,
I wonder whatever else may loom.
I wander to the toilet block,
It's funny cos the door's now locked.
There's something fishy going on,
I bet it's Joe again - or John!
I bend and peer under the door,
I see water trickling on the floor.
Someone will have their work cut out,
They'll need wellies - without a doubt!
So with whistle blown, it's one o'clock,
Let's try to get this door unlocked.
It's been a hectic sort of day,
We should have extra in our pay!
So with door unlocked - is there a burst?
Of course there's not - *it's April the 1st!*

Alison Jane Lambert

DOGGEREL!

My lovely dog, my true best friend,
Mongrel of high degree,
His head and body and his end
Match no known pedigree.

Such faith and loyalty and trust
Patch does bestow on me.
I want to give him all that's best
And more, if that could be.

I love long, sunny country strolls
When I let him run free
To chase rabbits . . . even voles,
And sniff each trunk of tree.

I am devoted to him;
You must be sure of that.
But windy, rainy winter walks?
I wish he were - a cat!

Susan Grant

THE SWINGING GATE

A gale was blowing and the gate was swinging,
We were homeward bound and happily singing.
As it was getting rather late
We thought we'd shut the offending gate.
I shut it gently and felt quite pleased.
We went a few yards and the latch had eased.
Back to the swinging with a click and a bang,
A challenge indeed for one of our gang.
'This is how you do it,' she said to me,
'Lift it a bit and then it'll be free.'
She lifted the gate and fell on top,
It had come off its hinges and she couldn't stop.
Her little round body went down with a thump,
Her legs were flailing, for she was quite plump.
We roared with laughter as she lay on the gate,
Forgetting completely it was quite late.
We hauled her back onto her feet,
Though the picture she made you just couldn't beat.
'That's it,' she said, 'the gate is staying
Right on the path where it is laying.'
We often wondered what the owners thought,
I'm pleased to say we never got caught!

Ruth Robinson

LIMERICK

One fine day in the middle of the night
Two dead men got up to fight
One had an arrow, the other had a gun,
One shot the other and said, 'What fun.'
Disappearing right out of sight.

Jean P McGovern

DRIVING LESSON

I thought I'd teach my girl to drive
Now I'm just glad to be alive
She'd had lessons and claimed to be good
This was not true, I soon understood.

When I asked if she knew which gear
She told me jeans and called me dear
Left and right were unknowns to her
This aspect gave me quite a scare.

Roundabouts had her mystified
She drove over one, I nearly cried
At traffic lights we caused a stir
Green came and went, she did her hair.

Confused the accelerator with the brake
Even a stronger man would quake
I know that I shall never again feel
Brave enough to get in if she's at the wheel.

P S D MacArthur

HEALTH CHECK

'Doctor, Doctor, I'm just not well,
I really don't know what to do.
My left leg, is giving hell.
So she sent me, to you.'

'I'm sorry your knee is so sore,
It looks big and you're in pain.
You said you have had it once before,
Well you've certainly got it again!'

'We'll do an X-ray for a start,
Smile now, don't be a wimp
And to be sure I'll check your heart
But don't forget to limp!'

'You have water on the knee,
There's not much we can do for that
But a plumber lives next door to me -
We will get you fitted with a tap.'

Douglas Bishop

YOU ARE WHAT YOU WEAR!

I worship designer labels,
People all gasp at my attire
This proves beyond question
That I am the person to admire.

I must be seen in Levi jeans,
In Versace and Prada I'm just cute,
I'm always shod by Jimmy Choo
And displayed in an Armani suit.

Enhanced by Tommy Hilfiger
My prestige can only grow bigger.
When I wear Dolce & Gabbana,
Then I feel that I live in Nirvana.

Since all labels are detectable,
I'm sure that my appearance is delectable.
Men never fail to make passes
When I sport my Gucci glasses.

I spend all my income on fashion,
But never regard it a waste,
It is invested to prove to the world
That I have such exquisite taste.

Jealous friends claim that I'm shallow,
Vain, pretentious and a freak,
But I never feel shame, only pride,
To be known as the geek with chic.

John B Morris

THE ELECTRIC TOOTHBRUSH

This newfangled dental contraption,
was bought as a whimsical reaction.
It has a big button to make it go,
and a smaller one to stop the flow.
Toothpaste starts frothing in the mouth,
going east to west and north to south.
Your lips around the brush you must keep closed,
or the froth sprays over glasses and up the nose.
You see, the brain at sixty doesn't work that well,
when thumb must choose 'tween big and small.
Without thinking, you remove to make certain,
and the mirror ends up like a net curtain.
Eventually getting the damn thing to stop,
I plump for a normal brush from the shop!

Joan Lister

I ONLY WANT TO PLEASE (TO TICKLE MY HUBBY'S FANCY I'LL STOP MY THONGS SWINGING IN THE BREEZE!)

Well I'm just a young housewife and love washing and ironing too:
And I'm ever so happy when I've got lots of housework to do.
Although I'm still a teenager, I got married at just seventeen,
There's something about polishing and cleaning, if you know what
                                                        I mean!
My darling hubby bought me a spin dryer and a washing machine too,
I've even got a dishwasher to save me time for other things to do.
Of course I have a vacuum cleaner and love booming and
                                        zooming around,
And there's something rather exciting at hearing its whining sound.
In fact I guess you could say that I've every domestic aid;
For as my hubby says to me, 'My sweet baby, you've got it made!'
To please him I always dress sexily, making sure I look just right,
In fact I'm always looking perfect for him from morning to night.
Even when doing my housework, I make sure I look beautiful too,
From my five-inch stilettos, high-cut thong and mini outfits, to my
                                        tattoos of red and blue!
My hubby is into body piercing and paid for me to be well pierced too;
I've had my belly button done, my nose, ears, tongue, and other
                                places where only he may view.
He says he likes to see me looking like a primeval girl to fulfil his
                                        fantasy dream
I really don't know what he means, he is an awful scream!
I have my minis cut high and slung low to show I'm hip and hot;
Showing loads of my bare midriff and the lovely, slinky hips I've got.
My hubby loves the way I try to please him by looking smart when
                                        I'm cleaning,
And sometimes I feel so happy, I almost think I'm dreaming.
There's just one thing that I love above all,
And it's the one thing that drives my hubby up the wall:
Because I only wear slinky thongs to show off my curvy behind:

For some reason my dearest, darling hubby doesn't want anyone else
To see them looking so fair and free, and he always says to me:
'Don't have your thongs hanging on the washing line, Jackie,
Where they're out there on show for all to see.
I don't want all the neighbours to see what you wear underneath,
You want to see how they natter and chatter with their bare teeth.'
So to keep the peace and not to turn my hubby into a rage,
I've decided to put my thongs in the spin dryer, as I'm a girl of my
own age.
I hang them up in the bathroom so no one can see but him and me;
And now we're both so happy with my thongs on or off, we're in
total ecstasy.

Jackie J Docherty

STAND UP! SIT DOWN!
(At a cinema in the 1950s)

I'm put behind big-headed bloke,
Enormous pipe with clouds of smoke.
An empty seat is farther down,
End of a row. I watch a clown.
Contented now. The film is nice,
Then Little Willie wants an ice.
Stand up and let the fellow by!
Sit down again. Another try!
The boy returns with ice in hand.
Stand up! Sit down! The film is grand.
The hero vaults a six-foot fence;
Then Little Willie wants the gents.
Stand up! Sit down! And off he goes.
When he comes back, treads on my toes.
Stand up! Sit down! I watch the screen
While Willie tells Mum where he's been.
His sister's jealous, plain to see,
So she decides she wants to wee.
Stand up! Sit down! She pushes past,
A longish wait, she's back at last.
Stand up! Sit down! I mop my brow.
Pray no more interruptions now.
Then I hear that Little Annie
Back is asking for a penny.
Stand up! Sit down! Is all in vain?
Stand up and then sit down again.
My neighbour now tugs at my sleeve:
He's seen it all, gets up to leave.
Stand up? Sit down? Not anymore!
I've had enough, make for the door.

F G Ward

GOLDEN OLDIES

Her:
I met him - I liked him - I married him,
I fed him - nurtured him - well I carried him
Silver - Pearl - Ruby - Gold
Once a shy bride - now a woman grown old.

Him:
I met her - I lusted - I *had* to marry her,
It was 'ring on finger' - or 'chastity barrier'.
Silver - Pearl - Ruby - Gold,
I will never admit - I'm a man grown old.

Her:
Dear Lord how we've laughed, and we've cried,
We've both had times when we've almost died,
Silver - Pearl - Ruby - Gold,
But we've pulled together - and together grown old.

Him:
Did you say *cold*, I'll get you warm,
Come 'ere me darlin', I'm in tip-top form,
B . . . the Silver – B . . . the Gold,
I'll chase you around till me little legs fold.

Her:
Oh! It's all in the mind - all in his head,
He's always asleep when I get in bed,
He's turned my hair silver - I've teeth capped with gold,
And I'm pretty damn sure - that we've *both* grown old.

Sylvia Fox

THE PERFECT SPONGE

I remember well that fateful day
I decided to take the plunge.
Armed with yet another recipe,
To make the perfect sponge.
I'd tried over and over again
But couldn't get it right.
It may sound like a fetish,
Or maybe even trite,
But I had made my mind up
To make the perfect sponge,
So once more, there I was,
About to take the plunge.
After all the mixing,
I found to my delight
That when I'd done the baking,
This time I'd got it right.
After displaying it with pride,
I left it to cool down.
I wasn't sure when I returned,
If I should laugh or frown.
There up on the kitchen bench
Sat Clyde, my fat black cat,
Having eaten half my sponge,
That was the end of that.
I fed the rest to the dog.
He really had a ball.
My dreamed of perfect sponge
Was a perfect memory, that's all.

Patricia Draper

RIB TICKLING

I have a small laugh
Which sits under
My seventh rib;
The one where
Adam never goes
And only Eve knows;

My laugh grows
When I
Am with you,
Rolls up into
A smile,
Bounces,
Giggles,
Opens up the
Muscles in
My face into
Curving crescents,
Makes my
Eyes dance.

My laugh
Grows louder,
When I
Am with you,
It is catching,
Enlightening,
Enhancing;

I think that
Laugh may be you.

Janet M Baird

TONGUE-TWISTED

'Twas choir practice, and the gathered medley
of members cheerily waiting
chattered and listened to news and views
and gently teased with good-humoured baiting.

One lady with humour and cheery smile
said she *always* sits near the men!
Another whose daughter to Fiji had gone
sparked an innocent verbal response as then . . .

someone's intention was honestly *meant*
to say, 'Fiji – *that's* quite *exotic*' -
but the intensity of the moment produced
roars of laughter to the sound of *'erotic!'*

'Twas choir practice, and the motley of members
in uproar of laughter still winging,
was called to order whilst excuses were made
for the staggered poor start to the singing.

No harm intended, the tongue-twisted member
put her all into keeping straight face
as, faces averted to concentrate better,
the choir finally found the right pace

to practice the hymns to be ready for Sunday,
and give of their best to the task
when the organist called them to order -
'Sing in *tune* in right *time* now, that's all I ask!'

'Twas choir practice and the motley gang gathered
succeeded to learn each new tune,
whilst the tongue-twisted dame will be forever reminded
of her 'age' and, perhaps, the full moon!

Ann Voaden

THE SHOOTING STAR

I saw a star the other night come falling to the ground.
Although I sought until daylight, no fallen star I found.
From high above, across the sky, a glittering, glowing spark,
It disappeared, a heav'nly fly, fluttering in the dark.

And all day long I wondered so, where could that star have gone?
Where could a startling spectre go, that in the darkness shone.
I thought and thought, but could not find an answer to my quest,
A cloud had swaddled 'round my mind, enveloping my chest.

So to an inn, to bandy there, with swineherds and the squire,
With stoups of ale and country fare, sack-possets and a fire.
A thousand shivers and a frown resided in the clan,
'You sure that star had come on down?' 'As sure as any man.'

''Tis funny that,' the squire opined, 'I ween 'tis very queer.'
A lording gent, whom form resigned ne'er pauper nor a peer –
''Tis troublesome, now see here chaps, the story's mighty thin,
If it had landed,' and he claps, 'it'd made a frightful din.

It'll probably have burnt a hole the size of Beam'ster Square,
And deeper than the Marshwood 'bowl' and plentiful to spare.
Why bless my beard, we'd all have been as burnt as morning toast.'
With that the swineherds grunt and grin, two teeth, one had the most.

'Well I only sees what I do see, I saw it all too clear,
Though what thee says, oh marry me, I would not now be here.
And now my friends, a stoup of ale, a jorum, or a jar,
For verily it must have been a spaceman in a car.'

D Haskett-Jones

OSCAR AND LUCINDA

Oscar one day fell down the stair -
He's currently in intensive care.
The plastic surgery was extensive,
But NHS, hence inexpensive.

Both legs were buckled, thus and so,
Horrendously - they had to go -
His head stove in like a ping pong ball
Or broken egg - and that's not all -

One arm was crumpled, a concertina,
He howled like a distressed hyena
Since it ruined the cut of his suit (Edwardian) -
The other resembled an old accordian.

His ribs collapsed like bowling pins.
His knees fetched up beyond his shins.
His chest imploded. His poor abdomen
Was cold and white, like a thawing snowman.

The surgeon, murmuring gravely, 'This'll
Be awfully delicate,' took his chisel,
His hacksaws, hammers, needles, thread,
And, hoiking Oscar out of bed,

Anaesthetised him on the table,
Reassembling as far as he was able -
With a tibia here, a femur there
And a brand new head of flaxen hair

The poor young lad whose accident
Had left him broken, bruised and bent.
Oscar, who suffered this distress
Has been rebuilt. No more, no less.

He'll wake up later, dazed and tender,
To start afresh, and called Lucinda.

Norman Bissett

ODE TO A BAR STEWARD

No amber nectar in the pumps,
The barrel has run dry:
And, staring at an empty glass,
The customer could cry.

The customer has his own glass,
Much cherished and well-used.
At the moment it stands empty
And he is not amused.

The customer is most upset
And can't wait here all day.
If there's no beer for him to drink
He'll soon be on his way.

The solution is quite simple -
If there is no refill,
The customer will walk away
And won't pay his bar bill!

Brian M Wood

THE DREAM AND AWAKENING OF A POLITICIAN

Oh! How I love to visit the zoo
And watch the elephant shave;
I love to watch the kangaroo,
Dressed as an Indian brave;
There's the hippo and the rhino,
Playing a game of chess
And performing on the piano,
The monster from Loch Ness.

There's a monkey in his cricket cap,
Drinking a cup of tea.
He has a giraffe upon his back
While climbing a sycamore tree.
The Vietnamese pigs are flying
And the lion is baking a cake,
While a polar bear is trying
To charm a rattlesnake.

Oh! Yes, how I love to visit the zoo,
It's there I can unwind,
And in my dream of fantasy,
My problems leave behind.
But tomorrow it's back to reality,
For that is my intent,
And attend that place of banality,
The mad house of parliament.

John Wells

THE BIG SLEEP

Now *Ovaltine* can help you sleep
Quite deep: to waken stronger.
But *nicotine* will make you sleep
Far deeper and much longer!

Peter F Ellison

MISHEARD

Aural
'Sex?' she asked him.
'Oh yes please,' he replied.
'You sleep next door and then we shout,
Knickers!'

Terry Wright

AN ELECTRIFYING EXPERIENCE

There was an electrician from Brixham
Who said my lights he could fix 'em.
There was a big flash, crash, wallop, bang,
Then in a loud, shrill voice he sang,
'The wires, you never should mix 'em.'

Janet Ramsden

THE SAD SAD TALE OF OLLIE BEAK

This is the tale of Ollie Beak,
Who went out seven nights a week,
To have such fun with all his mates,
And stay out very, very late.

They'd stay out 'til the crack of dawn,
And get home bleary-eyed and worn,
And sleep right through the live-long day,
They loved to live their lives that way.

One night, whilst out on the razzle,
Ollie's eyes went all a-dazzle.
He met a girl called Wendy Owl,
And said, 'Cor! You look tasty! Wow!'

His heart felt light, his tummy bobbly,
Further down, his knees went wobbly,
Ollie had never felt this way,
Hot and flustered, drunk and gay.

The truth was, Ollie was in love,
The playboy owl became a dove,
His mates meant nothing any more,
Or staying out 'til half-past four.

He went instead with Wendy Owl,
And told his friends, 'Don't cry or howl,
I've never felt this way before,
But now I do, I like it more.'

And so he told his mates goodbye,
And with a twinkle in his eye,
He courted Wendy, how they wooed,
His friends all thought him very rude.

But there was no one else for Ollie,
Wooing Wendy made him jolly,
Any time she wasn't there,
He sat and sulked in deep despair.

They'd go out nights and woo and woo,
And get home early (half-past two),
He'd put his wings around her neck,
And give her beak a little peck.

So Ollie's happy situation
Got discussed across the nation,
P'raps they would get married soon,
They'd met three months ago, in June.

They wooed and wooed as they had done,
Beneath the sultry summer sun,
And as the autumn settled in,
Our Ollie went and bought the ring.

The date was set, the guests invited,
Then all at once, their love was blighted!
Flash of lightning, crash of thunder,
Then the sky was rent asunder.

Then it belted down with rain,
You've never seen, nor will again,
So much water from the sky,
Nothing on the earth was dry.

And Wendy stood, all dripping wet,
Poor Ollie, soaked as he could get.
And that was when she broke his heart,
And told him they would have to part.

She said, 'I'm sorry, Ollie dear.'
As Ollie brushed away a tear.
'This is the end for me and you,
Because it is too-wet-to-woo!'

Mick Nash

THE WRONG ADDRESS

He drove with attention along the dark road,
The mist swirled about him as if hiding his load.
His load of manure - the richest he'd had
Was quite overwhelming - the baddest of bad.

The environment officer was done for the day.
After worries and troubles, he'd soon hit the hay.
Pollution, emission, the unblocking of drains -
Argument, protest - he felt mentally in chains.

Hello, what's this - a big load at his gate,
And the smell - oh my goodness (it was now in full spate).
What terrible person had done this misdeed?
He would have to remove it at double-quick speed.

At long last he contacted the firm in the case
And told them to get the load out of the place.
But threats did not worry the boss of the firm,
Usually he made the other chap squirm.

'We'll take it off when we're coming that way.'
'You take it now, or I'll see that you pay.'
The boss merely smiled a smile like a knife,
But he hadn't accounted for the environmental wife.

She appeared at his office with guns at the ready
And when she had finished, his hands were unsteady.
'Yes, Ma'am and no, Ma'am,' he bowed to her wishes,
It was almost as if he would wash all the dishes.

So the moral of all this is quite plain to see,
When you're stuck with a load that's not meant to be,
Send for the wife - she'll sort it out,
She just needs to look - there's no reason to shout.

Ronald Moore

CHANGING ROOM

I'm feeling hot and flustered
Getting in a state
The changing room nightmare
Has now become my fate.

To try on pairs of trousers
I'm standing on one leg
Can't seem to keep my balance
And fall out the door instead.

'Are you OK, Sir?'
The shop assistant enquires
With my trousers around my ankles
My street cred had expired.

The inside leg was short
A waist of thirty-four
Now six doughnuts later
I'm really not so sure.

I need to do some sit-ups
To get my waistband down
Or shall I just by hangers
And ease my trouser frown.

Now shock, horror, amazement
At last a pair that fits!
I stand back from the mirror
To resemble a bag of chips.

No need to bash the plastic
So avoid an assistant's grin
Go belt up your interest free credit
On trousers I just can't win!

John Carter

UNTITLED

A twit of a twat from Twerp 'ill
Reversed her g-string of scarlet and purple
Her flaps flared vermilion
But she didn't Brazilian
So on approach you could give her a fur pull.

Mark Fayle

MUSICAL ACCIDENT

A one-man band from Norway,
Went head-over-heels through a doorway,
His tongue jammed as he sang,
His banjo strings went twang! twang!
And his cymbals have been left in a poor way.

Carol Ann Darling

A GOOD DAY FOR HUNTING

The autumn leaves were falling fast
Grandad said, 'He'll soon be back
That tree rat with the bushy tail
This time I'll get him, I won't fail.'

He scoured the attic, cupboards too,
To find his weapon, far from new
The pellet gun had seen better days
He swore he'd be no longer plagued.

He found a rusty tin on high
From the garage he gave a sigh
With pleasure beaming on his face
He cleaned the gun with great haste.

He didn't have to wait too long
As he spied a tail, straight and strong
The squirrel committed the cardinal sin
When on his lawn he began to dig.

He opened the door with hunter's stealth
Loaded his weapon and cunningly knelt
Like Rambo then he took his aim
The quarry now was his fair game.

His finger slowly pulled the trigger
With a crack the pellet flew like a quiver
It travelled at least a metre's length
Then took a nosedive into the fence.

The squirrel ran with all his might
The noise gave him a heck of a fright
But Grandad swore he'd won the day
And far away the squirrel would stay.

But ever since that ground-breaking day
The squirrel though he wanted to play
So brings his family to have some fun
And play with Grandad and his little gun.

Gillian Mullett

MAN-BRAIN: A COMMISSION

Man-brain scratches at his balls,
Doesn't know how to rinse his smalls,
Changes his underwear once a week,
His briefs they stink and his socks they reek.

Man-brain, looking for an easy lay,
Slaps on Old Spice ready for the day.
Down the pub, pool to relieve his stress,
And won't say 'ring you' or give you his address.

Man-brain thinks only of his stomach
A couch potato, a great fat lummox,
Chillin' in front of his TV dinner,
Burger and chips, hopes he's getting thinner.

Man-brain eyeing up totty on the street
Don't give him a second look as they can smell his feet!
Loves tight skirts, breasts large and firm,
Likes curly hair as it matches his perm.

Sex and food and playing with his d**k,
Food, sex, scratching, God what a prick!
Sex, food, sex, sex, food,
Grubby little sh**e, you wouldn't want to see him nude.

Quite amazed why girls just leave,
Farting and belching, wipes his nose on his sleeve.
No free sex or food this week, what a shame!
Your d**k's too small mate, just like your man-brain!

E D Darling

THERE'S ROSEMARY

'There's rosemary, that's for remembrance.
Pray you, love, remember.'
Ophelia, Hamlet.

Remember. How could we forget
That colourful, disastrous vignette?

Stage left: stagger and fall.
Stage right: lines tumble and brawl
With the meaning of what was said
Against the speed with which they fled
From your mouth and fell empty
Onto the stage - scattered like debris.
Advice given in vain when someone
Kindly said, 'Don't ever dare to shun
The audience. Look to them and loudly
Decree every other word to such a degree
That no one can doubt your greatness.'
On the night, this method for success
Was the rope with which you gaily hung
Yourself. We, the audience, were stung
Into submission, as the words cannoned
Forth, laying low all in their wake, Fashioned
By nerve, addiction, rapidity, inability.
Your lines, like lethal weapons, freed
The soul of the play from the plot
That for centuries had bound it
To the page.

Nick Gander

IDENTITY

'Congratulations, you've got twin girls,' the midwife beams,
'Now what names are they to have?'
'Well, Ruth is one,' my mother exclaimed,
'But the other is eluding me, it seems.
What's your name?' she asks the nurse.
'Rita,' she exclaims.
'Well, that'll do nicely.'
But to this day my sister still blames
The nurse whose namesake she was lumbered with.

Could have been worse, it might have been Jezebel.
Think of going through life with that handle.
I apologise to those who do,
But what a narrow escape, that's true.
Ruth and Rita, the names blend so well,
But which is which, some say. I'm blowed if I can tell.
When on our christening day one godmother proclaimed
When asked by the vicar, 'What is this child to be named?'
'Rita!' she said, with all confidence ablaze,
Then looked in doubt when into the child's eyes she gazed.
'At least I think I've got it right.'
So all in all, I'm going through life
Thinking I'm Ruth, but try as I might,
I'm still not convinced that Rita isn't my name,
With Rita being Ruth. Confused?
Well, we feel the same.

Some day I'll write my memoirs
To describe my life as a twin,
And when I'm asked for a title of my book
I'll reply, 'There's only one which really fits in.'
'Please tell me the title, do.'
'Why of course, no other possibility. It has to be
Who's Who!'

Ruth Locker-Smith

SHEER PHOBIA

Do you suffer from philematophobia?
It's rare but it can occur.
Do you suffer from coulrophobia?
Not amusing even for a voyeur.
Do you suffer from pogonophobia?
The answer may seem quite weird.
These three problems put together
Add up to kissing a clown with a beard.

Do you suffer from opthalmophobia?
Not a sight to be seen.
Do you suffer from pteronophobia?
This can be very amusing and mean.
Do you suffer from chionophobia?
Perhaps the answer is no,
For this is surely unusual,
Being stared at while being tickled in the snow.

T A Napper

UNTITLED

This is a tale, but very true
About me and a vexing loo:

When we moved in, I thought it grand
I now have everything at hand
A brand new fridge, a cooker too
A bedroom, spare room and a loo.

But ever since I've graced its seat
It's left me with a shocking treat.
No sooner have I pulled the chain,
The damn *thing* comes up again.

Tony is a cavalier
He would not dream to give a sneer
'Don't sit too long, don't make it settle!'
He tells it kindly to his Petal.

But, whatever I do try,
It comes back, I don't know why?
With some Brobat I attack
Gave it with a stick a whack.

Boiled the kettle nicely hot
Chucked cold water, what a lot!
Then, at last, it fades away
Oh, thank heaven; what a day!

Will it bother me tomorrow?
I do wonder with some sorrow
And, in my commiseration
I shall opt for *constipation*.

If you think this is the end,
You'll be very, very wrong
Tony thought I ate cement
Or some other stuff, quite strong.

But it fired back on him
On a lovely Friday morning
As he spent more than a penny
It stayed put, without a warning.

Laugh we did, and laugh we do
Over our *vexing* loo
Will it go or will it stay?
We don't mind *it* either way.

Ursula Chaplin

OUR ROOM

It lingers in the corridor
It lingers in the classrooms
It lingers up and down the stairs
But stinks in our room

It really is an awful smell
I bet it's much nicer in hell
I think the person responsible
Should be ambushed and chucked in a well
Oh how it stinks in our room

I wish someone would say something
We haven't got a clue where to begin
But we can't take it much longer
Because my God, it stinks in our room

We are thinking of going on strike
Because we don't think it's right
To have to put up with such plight
So someone *please* do something
It really stinks in our room

SOS.

Pauline E Reynolds

RIB TICKLING MOMENTS

There was a young fellow from Brum
Who played tricks just for fun
A trick backfired on him one day
For this of course he had to pay
Sitting on a tube of superglue gum
He was stuck to the chair by his bum.

Trevor Beach

THE BULLY

Bang went the door
And the bully sat down.
Breaking every smile
With a scowl and a frown.

Full of self-importance
With every word to say
Too opinionated, puts
A damper on the day.

I look upon her in pity,
How lonely she must be.
No friendship is on offer,
Not even a cup of tea.

My office is a small one,
No room for a big head,
While I wait for that
Important phone call,

Saying, 'She won't be
Coming into work,
Because she's dead.'

Simon P Hewitt

A Slimmer's Tale

I really need to lose some weight,
My figure's in an awful state!
When my neighbour told of her 'wonder diet'
I thought, ooh, I think I'll try it.
Next day she came and brought the books
I said, 'After this biscuit, I'll have a look.'
So trying to muster some dieting thoughts,
I attempted to choose one; there were so many sorts.
With one hand thumbing through the magazines,
(The other opening a tin of beans)
I saw 'Fruit Only' - the one for me,
I'd begin it as soon as I'd had my tea!
Or 'The Low Carbohydrate', that looks fun,
I thought, tucking into a currant bun.
Next day I decided to do my best
And put my will-power to the test.
But by dinnertime my nerves were on edge,
And I knew I'd have to break my pledge.
As I read about Doreen, this year's slimmer,
I tucked into a hearty dinner.
At teatime I had a funny spell,
So I had to eat lots then as well.
As I undressed for bed I was nibbling a cake,
I was feeling hungry for goodness sake!
I stood on the scales and what do you know,
I still had another three stones to go!
I turned off the light with a feeling of sorrow,
Determined to start my diet tomorrow!

Rosemary Pooley

OUCH! HERE I GO AGAIN

I had a spell a while ago
Of falling flat on my face;
And hard as I tried to stay upright,
This was often not the case!

I wasn't under the influence,
Though I don't say no to a tot;
But no - I was always sober
And ouch! It always hurt a lot.

I've never been an elegant bird,
In fact clumsy's my middle name.
As a child I'd fall over a matchstick,
A potentially painful game.

On the way down the garden,
The dog rushes past;
Up go my legs -
I come down on my . . . !

I pull for work and get out of the car
And I'm facing the right direction
A minute later I'm sprawled on the floor
Whispering words I dare not mention.

I've grazed my knees, I've broken my jaw;
I've sliced my head on the warehouse door.
I'm not allowed in a china shop,
And I've masked my forehead on the doorframe - wop!

But there is an upside to this tale of woe,
It's the laughter I bring as - over I go!

Shirley Hillier

FAIRLY FOOTBALL

It's a funny old game, and was funnier still
At school - a real good laugh.
The classroom was the football pitch,
And the teams, well, they were the staff.

To score a goal, they must say a word
That teachers use quite rarely,
Not boot the ball in the back of the net,
But just use the little word 'fairly'.

So Maths Athletic met History Town,
And English played PE,
And every boy in the class wrote down
Each goal, with wondrous glee.

Those staff whose class control was poor,
When 'fairly' they had sounded,
Were cheered with a miniature 'Hampden Roar',
And truly were dumbfounded!

So keen was I to miss no score
From teachers' lips might pass -
The 'fairly' term was the only term
That I was top of the class.

The cup was given to Geography Town,
Whose teacher lived in Wellow,
As we sang to him in his old black gown,
'For he's a fairly good fellow'!

Alan Dudeney (The Poet Laurie-ate-for supper!)

MEMORIES OF MY YOUTH

In the sixties I enjoyed crazy parties,
Loud music and just as loud clothes.
Wore a beehive set hard with lacquer,
Black mascara smudged my eyes and nose.
My lipstick was pink and pearly,
My earrings were gaudy and big,
My skirts got shorter and higher,
Even though my legs looked like twigs.
All my shoes were pointed stilettos,
Miscellaneous colours so bright,
I teetered and tottered wherever I went,
And pan-sticked my face extra white.
I remember my jeans were much tighter,
My figure was slim and smart,
My skin was soft and silky,
Only innocence welled in my heart.
I could dance all day without resting
To that rock and roll music I adored,
With my blonde hair bleached whiter than ever,
Never knew what it meant to be bored.
Now flat shoes are needed for my bunions,
I've a bad back and specs extra thick,
I don't jive anymore, just prefer a hot bath,
And often I hear my hip click.
Still these memories are mine to hold,
And unlocking the key with pride,
I let people laugh with, or at me,
After all, this is still me inside.

Celia Auld

MAY YOUR GOD GO WITH YOU

His casual elbow on the bar,
His pompous stance, his equipage,
Pronounced to all here was the Tsar
Of this club bar-room's entourage.

Four times and more he held the floor
With unselfconscious arrogance,
Inferring with each raucous roar
His wealth, his power, his influence.

Stentorian he aired strong views
On every complex theme among
The unemployed, the crooks he'd choose
To be exiled and flogged and hung.

'A self-made man like me can't really
Get to where I am today
Being namby-pamby, touchy-feely.
I cut straight through and say my say!'

Just down the bar, an older man
Said, listening to the brash orator,
'I see you are a self-made man
Who clearly worships his creator!'

Patrick Brady

THE LOTTERY

I live in hope
of winning
something
some day
with my one pound coin.

Each week
foregoing milk
I pick my six
From over the shoulder
Of whoever's
In front.

No prophesied dreams
or schemes
made in
night computer classes.

Just me
foregoing cows
in hope
someday
of asses.

Simon Daniels

STEAMY GLASSES

A miserable wet day in November.
Quite a depressing scene.
Making my way to the doctor's,
To a place I'd never been.
Newly joined the civil service,
Required an eyesight test,
I'd declared I was short-sighted,
That is without my old specs.
Second-guessed the doctor's address.
The surgery was in a side street,
Beside St Peter's Church, Stoke.
Number 4 Brook Street, turned out to be a joke,
To me and other folks, an idiot's master stroke.
Me, rain-soaked, with my glasses like steamy windows,
The logic seemed to me, next to 2, number 4 would be,
For the rain obliterated the whole wet world to me.
Counted 2 - 4, then up the steps, through the door
To the reception desk situated on the first floor.
'I've come to see Doctor John for an eyesight test.'
Couldn't say more before the receptionist interjects.
'I though so pet, I might have guessed,
This is a solicitor's office. It's next door.
I hope you pass your sight test, luv,' the slightest laugh.
Apologised, off I stride, up next door's flight of steps.
In my haste, more disgrace, tripped to face the doctor
As he let out a patient through his front door.
A wet day double whammy, me floored once more.
Steamy glasses, as this day passes, earning jokes galore.
Me, creating a spectacle, as a youthful innocent abroad.

Jonathan Pegg

A VEGETARIAN COCKTAIL

PA had gone for the *snip,*
I liked them roasted myself,
PA had married a *swede,*
But now he was left on the shelf.

The *medley* of women had all been in vain,
A *batchelor's pea* he'd become,
He went to *brussels* in search of fame,
But he ended up with none.

A *chip* on the shoulder, was all he was left,
He felt *frozen, roasted* and *fried,*
For so long I tried to please them all,
His pitiful *pea* replied.

My *corn* is sweet,
My *brocci* don't *lie,*
He argued as he *steamed,*
I've been to *haricot* and *shallot,*
And I like my *potatoes* creamed.

As he ended his journey of veggie delights,
He thought he'd try *cauliflower* cheese,
But all those vegetarian bites
Just brought him to his knees.

Susan Jenner

JOHNNY ROUSE

I tell the sad story of poor Johnny Rouse,
Who fell from a ladder while painting his house,
He made very certain the paint was well mixed,
But forgot to make sure that the ladder was fixed.
He extended the ladder to reach its full height,
Directly above the bathroom skylight.
The window he wanted, he found with dismay
In spite of his stretching was too far away.
He leaned over further, extending his brush,
The ladder slipped sideways, then down with a rush.
As he fell through the skylight, he knew with dismay,
He'd ignored the first rule of painting that day.
The first basic lesson is always make sure,
Before you climb up, check the ladder's secure.

Roy Le Grice

HALLOWE'EN

I bought an orange pumpkin,
Cut out a mouth and nose,
Attached it to a body
And dressed it in smart clothes.

I placed it in a pentacle,
Chanted an ancient spell,
Called up the Prince of Darkness
From the fiery hobs of Hell.

I conjured up the Devil
To grant me what I craved.
He sat there with his long, forked tail
And was very well behaved.

'I'll grant you what you ask for,
But I expect a fee.
I want your soul forever,
Sign here if you agree.'

I signed and made the contract,
He vanished from my chair,
But I had my heart's desire,
A man with ginger hair.

Molly Price

BODY PAINT

(When chocolate body paint first appeared in the shops, in my innocence, I didn't realise what it was for!)

This is the tale of Betty May, who, waking up on Christmas Day
Discovered something in her stocking which you perhaps
may think quite shocking!
But Betty's face flushed deepest pink. 'Oh Bob,' she breathed
and gave a wink,
'This present really is so quaint. You've given me
chocolate body paint!'
Her husband said, 'Perhaps you might use your body paint tonight?'
'No, not tonight,' said Betty May. 'I'll try it out on Boxing Day . . .'

When on cold turkey they had fed, Bob said, 'Shall we go up to bed?'
Betty answered, 'Later dear, I've got too much to do, I fear.'
At last - 'I've done it!' Betty called. (Bob, her husband, was enthralled)
But slightly disappointed too. 'I thought I'd do it dear, for you,'
He said, as he leaped up the stair to their boudoir - she was not there!

Then, from the drive he heard her shout, 'Bob, darling,
are you coming out?
Come and see what I have done. I've really had a lot of fun!'
Bob could not credit what he saw - what she had used his present for!
'My car was looking rather shoddy. Your paint was lovely for its body.'
(In ecstasy, their old dog Rover, licked the mini car all over.)

Kath Hurley

A GIGGLE

Holidaying with my son on his yacht,
My age I temporarily forgot.
The rail at the bow was rather high
But to get off onto land, I had to try.
In the crowded marina it was quite a manoeuvre,
Now I'm the 'gal' who couldn't get her leg over!

H M Birch

THE ADDICT

I must admit I have an addiction,
I'm taking pills of every description.
Some of them are on prescription,
But alternative medicine, that's the attraction.
I read all the bumph and I'm hooked - to distraction!

Big brown bullets for circulation,
Tiny whites for dehydration,
Yellow tablets for constipation.
The choice is really quite extensive,
Can't take them all - it's too expensive.

Two-tone ovals for hypertension,
Pills to settle indigestion.
Pills for things I'm loath to mention!
If I'm depressed and feeling fearful,
There are pills to make me bright and cheerful.

Water pills for irrigation,
Pills for joints with inflammation,
Pills to help my concentration,
Pills for libido, whatever that is!
Don't think I've got it. Give it a miss.

Pills that will rejuvenate
All the things degenerate,
Give me life, resuscitate,
Make me frolic, frisk and caper,
Well, that is what it says on paper!

I wonder if, perhaps one day,
I'll take a good look at myself and say,
'I'm going to throw all these pills away.'
After much thought, I've reached a conclusion -
It's all a matter of self-delusion!

Hannah Leventhall

RED RIDING HOOD REVISITED

We all know the story of Red Riding Hood.
She visited Grandma, who lived in the wood.
Sent by her mother, her father knew too,
Is this something responsible adults would do?
They're dysfunctional . . . need training . . . in new parenting skills.

She soon met a wolf as she walked down the road,
He talked to her kindly, said he'd carry her load.
And she told him her business. Would a nice girl do that?
It's a *wolf* for heaven's sake, not a tame pussy cat.
She's on the pull . . . dressed in red . . . up for it.

The wolf ran to Grandma's, he liked his meat rare,
So he gobbled her up, then began to prepare
To receive his new friend, she would be his next meal.
As I write this I worry, I can't help but feel
It's an eating disorder . . . Bulimia? Needs counselling . . . his own
social worker.

He dons Grandma's nightie and jumps into bed,
He seems to enjoy it. It has to be said
He's into cross-dressing. Does it give him a thrill?
He'll meet our Red in bed, I don't think she's his meal.
He's into lingerie . . . white . . . voluminous . . . all encompassing
. . . wow!

The woodman comes in and kills our wolf dead.
Now I hate to take sides, but it has to be said
Talk could have resolved this in some other way.
I really don't see why the poor wolf should pay.
He's a victim . . . a minority . . . an endangered species.

They could even have married, or at least lived in sin,
Well, I'm not really sure if marriage is in.
With children and in-laws, a mortgage to pay
And our Red to nag him, he'll soon mend his ways
And they all lived unhappily ever after . . . just like us.
Well, what do you think this is? A fairy story?

Ann Wood

LACK OF SLEEP

I saw a funny thing one day, while passing through the town
As I strolled along the main high street, two large seagulls were down
They reminded me of a married couple, as one stared in a shop
I stood within six feet of them, the sight did make me stop.

One, inside a shop entrance, was staring at its own reflection
The other made a raucous noise, not making out the connection
I wish I'd had a camera with me, it would have made a sight
But not as beautiful as watching them, when they are in full flight.

They sit upon the roofs of these flats, and there they boldly stare
At nothing in particular, just glaring here and there
They swoop across the sea each day, their beaks sharp as a spear
But from our roofs on summer mornings, I wish they'd disappear!

They are amazing really these birds, they never sit on trees
On buildings all around the town, on roofs and chimneys
Not scared of anything these birds, they will defend their nests
But to people of many coastal towns, they're a bunch of flamin' pests!

In summertime when dawn is early, they wake me at half-past four
By midday at the latest, my head is terribly sore
I sit and watch and call them names, I cannot mention here
If I could get so close to one, I'd kick it up its rear!

They might be an awesome sight to watch, as winds carry them
across the sky
I wish they'd clear off somewhere else, I'd prefer some more shut-eye!
I'm sure all my local neighbours would agree wholeheartedly on this
To be able to sleep until seven am, it would be pure bliss.

I know I'm sounding paranoid, but their eyes hold an evil leer
I'd like to try and cast a spell, and make them disappear
That flamin' horrible noise they make, it's a non-stop flippin' racket
If I see one on the street again, I'm sure I'll try to whack it!

So excuse me now, I have to go, I need to close my eyes
Before a flock of these giant birds, comes swooping from the skies!

B W Ballard

THE HYPOCHONDRIAC

Dear Doctor, I am full of woe
I've such a pain in my big toe.
I know you'll also sympathise
About the ache in both my eyes.

On my leg, red spots abound,
I hope a cure is quickly found.
They itch and burn and cause me grief,
Oh how I long for some relief.

Fingers squashed by door on bus,
Make me want to swear and cuss.
Now with fingers bruised and bent,
I'd love to give my anger vent.

But I must banish thoughts of ill
And hope to get a magic pill.
So when I close your surgery door
I'll be recovered, that's for sure.

Ivy Stewart

JUST MY LUCK

I wrote odes and sonnets
And the odd clerihew
Just the way most poets do
When my publisher rang
To tell me I was fired
It seems that my poetic licence
Had expired.

Dai Blatchford

THE BUNNET BANDIT

The bunnet bandit, aged 73
Sad to say is married to me
His moans and groans I take in my stride
His 'escapades' don't dent his pride
The explanation's plain to see
It's not his fault, it's down to me
The telly's too loud, his plate's too full
Who hid his glasses under the stool?
A haircut seems a simple task
What could go wrong? You may well ask
I heard a commotion and there he was
Shouting the odds and arguing the toss
He'd picked up the wrong bunnet, surprise, surprise
The rightful owner was mesmerised
I apologised, we made a hasty retreat
Out of the shop and into the street
Victor Meldrew is not dead
He's alive and sleeping in my bed.

Catherine Hislop

MEAT AND TWO VEG!

With great feeling he was up there reeling
As the pipers droned the highs and lows
With gay abandon he looked grand on
The stage at one of the Highland shows
Nearby gazing a young girl lazing
As she watched him twirl to a lively reel
No escaping, her mouth now gaping
She was appreciating his wide appeal
Sunbathing lady had moved to place shady
As the pipers played a well-known lilt
And had seen right up that Scotsman's kilt!

Jon EL Wright

RELIGION, LEGEND AND MYTH: THE ART OF CULTURAL OSMOSIS

Myths flow lazily across the soft membranes of our lives,
religions in essence are fundamentally the same,
and legends are the lovers of literature and lies.

Here, have a cup of cultural cocktail.

David slings a well-slung shot and Godzilla drops down dead
Sirens sing a well-sung song and Homer picks up his pen.
Prometheus, that cheeky guy, stole fire from the gods.
He should have no regrets, for his reason was great:
it was to light James Dean's cigarette.

Here, have another; it will show you what was who.

Across the sky, whilst singing spectacularly high,
on a white horse came Marilyn riding.
With a Boop Boop De Doop, she scoops Shiva up
and bare-a**sed, bareback they go flying.
She takes the war god past Mount Olympus,
to a pub that is known as Valhalla.

Are you feeling tipsy? Have one for the road.

Goodbye Jason and your Argonauts, your time is up,
Maradonna and the Argentines have usurped your place,
using the Hand of God in their quest for the golden cup.
And Robin Hood steals arrows from Cupid,
to make the rich fall in love with the poor.

Please, don't be sick near the poem.

The tri-pronged fork of Lucifer - religion, legend or myth?
Two-horned head of the Minotaur - myth, religion or legend?
A bi-pronged sword called Zulfikar - legend, myth or religion?

You are looking slightly miffed.

Stories and religion, legends and myths,
across race, country and time these fictions exist.
They bring us together; show that we're the same.
Why do we do it? The reason is vain.
We fictionalised history to hide the truth,
we're all just monkeys who faked our roots.

You're drunk.

Chris Williams

RED FOR DANGER

I went down to London
With my brother Jim,
When someone flung
A tomato at him.

Now tomatoes are soft
And do not bruise the skin,
But this bugger did,
It was still in the tin.

Edna Gosney

A WINDY DAY

The wind plays like a naughty boy -
tugging at tired fences,
then pushing over dustbins
and tossing litter all about.

The wind plays like a naughty boy -
pulling at women's hats and
turning umbrellas inside out,
before opening garden gates.

The wind plays like a naughty boy -
throwing school work on the ground,
then giving kids the run around,
blue ink runs when a puddle's found.

The wind plays like a naughty boy -
scattering leaves near railway lines,
just to make the passengers late.
Pulls a weak branch to hear it break!

The wind plays like a naughty boy -
whistling as women walk by
struggling to hold dresses down,
people smile as the women frown.

Olliver Charles

THE CROCODILE

His coat is horny, scaled and tough,
Made of the most obnoxious stuff.
Atop his head those bulging eyes
Look at you in feigned surprise.

Now this, of course, is just a ruse -
A stratagem he likes to use
To ambush victims at his will,
Then come in quickly for the kill.

His legs are short, his tail too long.
He waddles as he walks along,
And though he is so somnolent,
He has an odious temperament.

He's no Adonis, to be sure,
But when he's frisky he can lure
A willing lady crocodile
To entertain him for a while.

This tropical, amphibious beast
Is always ready for a feast,
So keep away from floating logs,
Adrift in croc-infested bogs.

For each of this insidious breed
Believes in the ignoble creed
That while he lives he has to bite
All moving things that come in sight.

His jaws are made to snap and crunch
His breakfast, dinner, tea and lunch.
For him, endowed with teeth like tusks,
Tibia bones provide his rusks.

So if you venture to the swamp
Where these reptilian creatures chomp,
Shoot your rifle and you could win
That perfect prize - his precious skin.

Celia G Thomas

AN ELDER

A man of say ninety-three
Went to climb down on one knee,
By the time he got there,
The young lady got scared
And ran off with a sailor to sea.

Michael D Bedford

BACK PROBLEM

'Have you tried stretching flat
To gaze up at the ceiling?
You could try the mat,
Or is bed more appealing?'
I'd 'done in' my back,
Couldn't sit down or rise,
It felt like the rack
That I'd tried on for size!
There's nothing more boring
Than scanning the roof,
So I'm now exploring
A new designer spoof.
Painted ceilings are a must
When lying here supine.
It's Mike Angelo or bust
Till I can rise and shine!

Evelyn Balmain

CHRISTMAS DAY LASTS FAR TOO LONG

Oranges aloft
Lo and behold,
Santa Claus is coming to town.
Not this year,
Probably not even the next,
But only when that wretched boy has taken his
Skate blades off our carpet.

Aunt is preparing
A side dish of irony,
If only they'd stop incessantly recalling the war,
Never mind, we've still got the dogs.

Step-gran is hosting,
With the most lavish tights you've ever seen,
Hell-bent on reinstalling order,
But the dogs aren't that keen.

So now on to charades,
A game so undervalued.
We all take part in sequence,
Demonstrating the lousiest yarn or song,
Or a film old enough to have an urn.

As Uncle lights another cigar,
The younger family jeer,
It's all become symptomatic
Of our annual Christmas cheer.

Anthony Cocking

LOVE POEM

(If I write you a love poem, can I come back in?)

Winsome, when the mouth is shut
A pouty look, a lip that juts
A profile for the proffered kiss
A flicker smile in case you miss

The queen of quiet, I do declare
Of tolerance beyond compare
Compassion if you're in distress
'Bless you,' if you make a mess

O gentle, dulcet tone of voice
O soothing purr, like Rolls Royce
Gold daffodil in full allure
Slim, elegant . . . manicured!

Kind to horses, kind to beasts
To cats when wind is in the east
A pillar of society
Whose children swear with piety

Many opposites, all in one
Exasperating, half the fun
Fully female, other half
Professed romantic, makes oi laugh!

(Okay, so I'll sleep in the tool shed tonight, then.)

Brian Henry

Love Found In The Heart Of His Bottom

A cowboy rode in side-saddle butt sore from Gdansk
With an abscess throbbing and glowing in his leather hide pants
Drowning his discomfort in the saloon with whisky
To the delight of the feminine barman, seeing him go painfully frisky,
And looks willingly and admiringly, removed his boil, called Lance.

Philip Roberts

CONFUSED

I got up in the morning
And took a midnight stroll,
When I saw a gunman fighting,
With a yellow pole.
There isn't anybody that I could say I know,
But I have loads of mates.
My life I have lived for thirty years,
And tomorrow I'll be eight.
I think I'll walk to town today
In my new red car.
It's only around the corner,
And really, really far.
I'm feeling wide awake now,
I think I'll go to bed
And put my new blue nightie on,
As I like the colour red.

Mandy Jayne Moon

JACK'S MOTHER

I asked Jack,
'How's your mother?'
He said,
'I've housed her in a
nursing home.'

Amarjit Bhambra

THE BALLET CLASS MONOLOGUE

Hold the barre gently please,
Plié now and bend those knees,
And Sara don't tease
David,
While he springs up high,
And Jack come down, you cannot fly,
Shut the window, blow your nose,
And Jenny please point your toes,

Lift your foot off the floor,
Dennis do not kick the door,
And Emily do not show your . . .
Teddy,
To Daisy-May,
Yes I know she wants to play,
All hold hands and gallop around,
And let's try not to make a sound,

Devant and derriere
Please put down that chair,
That plant is falling please beware,
Katie,
Do not tread on it . . . no!
Now your ballet shoe has a black toe,
Turn around, do not spin,
Arms above your head, not under the chin,

Put the waste bin down and sweets away,
I really have had enough today,
Whatever will your mother say?
Jodie,
Let's all curtsey now,
And boys, let's see you bow,
Next week will soon be here,
But will I? No fear!

Ann G Wallace

THE YOBBO

I saw a little yobbo, sitting on a wall,
I said, 'Hey little yobbo, be careful not to fall.'
He glared down at me, and with a nasty grin, said,
'Bugger off and leave me, or I'll smash your face right in!'
I knew not why he hated me, so turned to walk away,
Wondering if I should feel sorry for him, having a bad day.
I couldn't find an excuse for his unpleasantness and wrath,
So turned around and smiled . . . then pushed the yobbo off!

Lance Honour

UNTITLED

I went to bed on Christmas Eve
And waited for Santa to come.
After he hung up my stocking,
I thought it was shocking
He got into bed with my mum.

Christmas comes just once a year
And now it makes me shed a tear.
I miss my toys and Christmas fun,
What a shame, I'm eighty-one.

When we went to the stores
To see Santa Claus,
He said, 'What would you like?'
I said, 'A new bike
And some ear muffs,
Cos Daddy snores.'

Leslie Newcombe

I HAVE A LUMP

I have a lump!
Somewhere I won't show,
No! You can't look,
It's you know, down below.

So off to the doctor's,
'Twas the only place,
Then to the specialist,
To visualise the case.

There an old nurse
Said, 'Off with your gear.
You can leave on your undies,
Well, for a while dear.'

Then in came the specialist
With a young nurse in tow,
Where could I look?
I didn't know!

'Down with your pants,'
Guess what came next?
He only instructed the nurse
To hold up me vest.

He made a remark
Like, 'What's the blush for?
Have no fear son,
We've seen it all before.'

Thank goodness it was ages,
Before the big carve,
On waking I said,
'You've cut me in half.'

Don't be disheartened
By this little tale,
For it's on the story
Of a very young, shy male.

Violet Cook

YOU KNOW WHO

When you watch your savings dwindle
carefully paid-for pension's gone
You Know Who's in on the swindle
adding taxes one by one . . .

Enacting yet more stupid law
to make Great Britain Europe's 'Shill',
thought up in Brussels by the score
You Know Who'll pass them still.

They don't care if you're too old
and saved some cash for when you're lax
You Know Who will leave you cold
and steal it with another tax.

And when you die the 'Red Flag' thieves
will all ensure an empty pot.
You'll find there's nothing left to leave
'cause *You Know Who* has nicked the lot.

D G W Garde

A BOY FROM DOVER

There was a young man from Dover,
Who dreamed of nothing but green clover,
Who was wise, witty and grim,
And who liked to tease and make fun,
At all his friends bathing in the sun,
Where he would watch and laugh,
As he drank his early morning gin,
So stupefied at the colour of their skin,
He would talk non-stop, with a rhyming giggle,
And he would throw in a surprise as well.

To any available lady, he would say,
'I've brought you a lucky green clover,'
For he wished a sweet kiss from her two lips
On his meddling sojourn from Dover,
For when he closed his eyes, she disappeared from sight,
Leaving him quite embarrassed and sober.
But this did not stop our wayward lad,
Not in the slightest way imaginable,
For inside his pocket, he always carried his green clover,
Hoping it would bring him luck, all the way from Dover.

So he carried on with his unwise musings,
Learning nothing from his sad experience,
When the second lady said, 'Are you from Dover?'
'Oh yes,' he replied, 'but this time, I've forgotten my green clover.'
'Green clover,' she answered cleverly, whilst blushing inside,
'Are you not that silly billy, that thinks luck is on his side?'
'Oh, you are a clever lady to have realised,
That I must be the unluckiest boy alive.'
And he continued with his quest, until he met a third lady,
Who simply died of fright.

James Stephen Cameron

WRITING A LIMERICK

I think for my next trick
I'll write a limerick
Putting pen to paper isn't easy
And the effort makes me queasy
I'll read it quick - before I'm sick.

Rosemary Davies

MISTAKEN IDENTITY

A zoo had a strange-looking tiger,
Whose stripes weren't complete - only dots;
And when I asked the keeper about it,
He replied, 'That's a leopard, you clot!'

Roger Williams

HOLIDAY

The time is near, only a week to go
you've worked hard for this all year,
two weeks of sun and relaxation
not to mention sumptuous food and beer.

Cases packed full to overflow
to the airport you now will head,
with a spring in your step, 'til you see the queue,
now you've a heavy heart and feet like lead.

Never mind, you'll eventually check-in
then to the bar for a drink or two,
you've remembered, you don't like flying!
So now you'd better have a few.

You're soon in the air above the clouds
knuckles white as you clutch the seat,
you've already seen the in-flight movie
at the cinema, only last week.

Touch-down, you breathe out a heavy sigh
the flight wasn't too bad after all,
not compared to the sweltering heat
you've to stand in at the luggage hall.

'Take it easy in the sun,'
the travel rep calls in vain,
you didn't listen, you're *lobster red*
and walking like John Wayne.

Dicky tummy over, you're just settling down
this past week has really just flown,
you'd best get out and enjoy yourself
as next week you'll be heading home.

Oh, the sheer delight of a holiday
it's now ended and you feel a bit sad,
only because it was a *disaster*
and you need another to get over the one you've *just had.*

Irene Reid

TO THE PENNINE NEWS

'Is that advertising?
I need an experienced man,
Immediately,
For the small holding.

Fit, strong and capable,
Used to American bison,
My birthday present
From America, a whole herd.

I have a high fence,
Electrified, which should be alright,
At least I thought so,
But now there's this shadow which shows
Through the lounge curtains.

Bumping the wall too,
This huge, shaggy bison outside,
Perhaps it's angry,
Or homesick, can you send someone?

Yes, it's rather late,
But I thought you might know someone
Who would come tonight,
Well, because I'm afraid of it.

This is my number,
But stay in the car on the road
Until you get a text,
In case they are all in the drive.'

Kathleen M Scatchard

THE CAT WHO CRIED

There was a cat who cried,
The next day she died.
She died in Devon
And went to Heaven.

> She cried in the day, she cried in the night,
> None went near her in case she'd bite.
> She was old and always moaned,
> She loved it best to groan.

> There was a cat who cried,
> The next day she died.
> She died in Devon
> And went to Heaven.

Laura Wilson (10)

LOVELY CLARE

I know a young girl called Clare,
Who had lovely, long, blonde hair.
With eyes full of lust
I looked at her bust
And thought, *Ooooh! What a lovely pair.*

Alan Weston

ROSI ATE THE ODOUR EATERS

My ex had really smelly feet
He wore Odour Eaters all day long
Rosalind was our German Shepherd
Sad was her partiality to tootsie pong.

The ex rose for an important day
Put on his clad and about to don his shoes . . .
Whoever had my Odour Eaters must *now* say!
Lack of response left him far from amused.
Rosalind, unable to conceal her guilt
Beneath her gigantic paws she nestled her head
With sheepish eyes the beans were spilt!
Soon remains were found hidden in her bed.

News out of the ex grump's grief
Sparked humour in the street
You see everyone loved Rosalind
Even those who feared the breed
Confidence to all she sowed the seed.

Canine girlies often eat what should be binned
And rid the unpalatable at its most
But yuk, his Odour Eaters Rosalind,
That was going one further than gross!

Rhoda Ann Woodford

ME A MISERABLE GIT

J K Rowling, yesterday I shot her
That's the end of that silly Harry Potter
Fancy a silly kid in a pointed hat
Have you ever seen such a spoilt brat?
In a box I do trap Bugs Bunny
Sell him to the takeaway for lots of money.
I see them go off in a hurry
Bet he ends up in a very nice hot curry.

Enid Blyton, I chop up her body,
No more of that silly kid Noddy.
If anything's to bring me to tears,
It's that kid and his fat friend, Big Ears.
To the kebab shop I sold Donald Duck,
Into some pan old Donald they chuck,
Gave him to some kid in a roll,
That will help him fill up a hole.

A A Milne yesterday, I covered in cement,
In a kiln Winnie The Pooh I sent.
That is the end of stupid Tigger
Another cat that won't grow any bigger.
I throw a net over Orville The Duck,
One by one his feathers I pluck.
His body with oranges I duly stuff,
One cooked duck is never enough.

Colin Allsop

MY MOUSE AND I

Once upon a midnight dreary,
I waited for my boyfriend weary,
I sat alone, gently rocking,
When suddenly there was a knocking.

I saw a mouse on my floor,
My knees were knocking, he was taking score,
My boyfriend came, so big and strong,
But I *was* really, really wrong.

He jumped up high upon a chair
And screamed at me, 'There's a mouse there.'
He's not my boyfriend, not any more,
Cowardice I just can't explore.

My eyes screwed up, my belly knotted,
Flying downwards the mouse I spotted,
Then my boyfriend, I showed him out,
Cowardice! Never more I want. I shout.

Now the mouse and me are best of friends,
We will stay united until the end.
Now upon a midnight dreary,
I wait no more for boyfriends weary.

Now my boyfriend is a mouse,
He lives with me in an old house,
I've made him a home on the floor,
My little mouse can't ask for more.

Joyce Healy

UNTITLED

She's got rings on her fingers
And rings on her toes
Her nipples
Her tummy
And even her nose
Most parts of her body
She's had pierced for years
And I do hope one day
She'll get round to her ears.

Brian Thomas

A LAMENTATION

I'm a lump where a lump shouldn't be
I thought I was hidden away
Snug and sideways concealed
When some nosy parker with a big machine
Said, 'Oi you, you shouldn't be there.
I'll tell the boss, he'll want you displayed
And shown for all to see.'
I cursed to myself and muttered inside,
A lump can live where it will, I say,
And shouldn't be stripped of his pride.
Leave me alone, I'm comfy and set
And progressively increasing my size.
He was told, inspected me well,
'There,' he said with glee,
'Is a lump where a lump shouldn't be.'
I heard all this and swelled with joy
Expecting the praise to land,
When to my horror I heard him say,
'This is a lump where it shouldn't be
And that I cannot allow.
Tomorrow we will burrow deep
And up he'll pop with a thud.'
Imagine my horror and grief,
My panicky striving to leave!
But all in vain! He whittled me out
And left me soggy and cold.
Now I'm a lump where a lump shouldn't be
But it's desperately uncomfy out here,
I miss my nice warm cosy digs
And wish I'd never been seen,
And allowed to continue my job in life
As a lump where a lump shouldn't be!

G J Pledger

TRUE STORY

There was a young lady called Jean,
Having a granddaughter one day was her dream,
Until one day
Her kids went away
And brought three grandsons onto the scene.

Christine A Smith

WHAT THE HELL!

Every time I come here,
the magic draws me ever near.
Feeling a bit ill,
but I'm in Cannes,
so what the hell!
Soaking up all that French chic,
sorry Bournemouth,
Torquay and Newquay,
but you're just taking the mick!

Anthony Welsh

MENU

Stuffed with gravy sauce . . .
>Roasted chicken curry.

Carrots, Brussels sprouts . . .
>Stir fried in a hurry.

Honey-leaking pancakes . . .
>Bubbling tasty texture.

Melting, sticky ice cream . . .
>Gifted from nature.

Oh, the choice that one can take . . .
>In the breakfast preparation.

Yet a simple jam on toast . . .
>Can also please the nation.

Elena Uteva

I'M NOT MOVING

I went off to do some shopping,
'Won't be long,' I said.
When on my return, these men were chopping
This sign into my flower bed.
'What's going on, young man?
My house isn't for sale, you fool.
Pull it down,' I scream and slam,
Phone the agents, trying to keep cool.
'My house is not for sale,' I shout down the phone,
'This is 11 Douglas Road, and we don't want to move.'
'Please accept our apologies, we've mistaken your home,
It's 11 Douglas Avenue that's selling,' she tries to soothe.
Well the funny part was, the poor lady was dead,
They'd mistaken the road markings and
Put my house up for sale instead.

Ann Hathaway

GOSSIPING MOTHERS

I was quietly sitting in the park the other day,
Watched some mothers who had brought their children there to play.
They were gossiping there together, their children, forgetting,
Till they fell into the lake and got a very good wetting.
Of course it was the children's fault. They had to take the blame.
Their mothers dashed in boldly and got a wetting the same.
Now all this goes to show, that whatever you have to do,
You must keep your mind on it, or this may happen to you.

Their dear little offspring got it, plainly in the neck,
They had to be hurried home, their clothes were dripping wet.
But if there had been a boy with them, this thought just made me grin,
The mothers would have been furious and blamed it all on him.

Now this is all so very true, it always is the same,
No matter what the trouble is, the men always get the blame.
It doesn't matter what we do, however much we strive,
We have to be at the beck and call of all our perfect wives.
Now don't screw up this paper, if you're tempted so to do,
Just think of your poor husbands and what they have to go through.
Just feel sorry for him sometimes, the cross he has to bear,
Try kissing him on the back of his neck, to show you have a care.

Albert E Bird

THE CLEANING LADY

You know I'm a cleaning lady, I pass by every day.
Dusters, polish and feather flicks, I carry on my way.
I clean away the memories of what was last night's meal,
I wash the floors and buff them, you can see your face so real.
I know lots of your secrets, the things you try to hide,
I know what you are really like, when doors are closed inside.
I know when you are happy, I know when you are sad,
Your house has little secrets, to tell me it's so glad.
She tells the one who loves her, who cares and makes her shine,
The only one who gives her lots of special time.
She looks forward to my visits, to make her look brand new,
Her windows are all gleaming, she now can see the view.
With the rubbish all cleaned out, her bins smell clean and fresh,
Wait until the family return to make another mess.
She cries and sighs, why leave the house this way?
Only to be told, the cleaning lady comes today.

Margaret Berry

A YULETIDE BALLAD TO BALLERT ORTHOPEDIC

Four days before Christmas and all through the shop
Not a creature was working, not even the mop.

The boss was in Northbrook, a-balancing his books
He had ledgers for braces and ledgers for hooks.

The year had been tough but the year had been good
And most of the workers had done as they should.

But for those who had chosen to sing their own tune
Their Christmas vacation had come a bit soon.

James Rasmusson

MOTTO OF THE INCORRIGIBLE NE'ER-DO-WELL

If you've nothing to say - then say it!
If you've nothing to do - just do it!
If you've nothing to find
Not a thought on your mind
And nowhere to go - go to it . . . !

If a task cannot wait - delay it!
If there's no time to lose - next-day it!
Should you wish to aim high
Simply measure the sky
That's called playing the fool - so play it . . . !

When a dream won't sit still - instil it!
Time was made to be killed - so kill it
If TV or a book
Lets your mind off the hook
It won't hurt you to look, then - will it . . . ?

If you've no course to stay - then stay it
There's a dead horse to flog - so flay it!
Though you feel down and out
You're still in with a shout
You just haven't a prayer - so pray it!

Whatever anyone said - you knew it!
When the line should be drawn - they drew it
Aimlessness was such bliss
Give ambition a miss
So lie back and give up - you blew it . . . !

Joanna Jay

IN THE WINK OF AN EYE

I think I was but six or seven
When Uncle George was called to Heaven
'He's happy now,' my mum had sighed.
'Your Uncle George got up and died'
I remembered days he wasn't dead.
Six-foot-four at least some said.
Eighteen stone I'd heard them say,
A big gruff Mick set in his way.

Mum said his innings had been long,
Yet in my logic thought Mum wrong
For I never knew him play the game
Cricket for him was far too tame
I knew he'd boxed within the ring
I'd heard the praises people sing
And how he'd then gone off to war
And medals won he proudly wore.

He used to scare me just a mite
A huge great man who filled my sight
Who'd put a docker's tongue to shame
'It was the war,' my mum explained
'We'll pay our last respects,' said Dad
'Your Aunty Mary's very sad
The wake to start at half-past three
Want a ride with Mum and me?

It's up to you - do what you like'
So I told them I would go by bike
For it really wasn't all that far
As Mum and Dad got in the car
Soon on Mary's door I knocked
Told her sorry for her loss
Then she did point to Uncle George
All laid out inside the porch . . .

'Go and kiss him, son, goodbye
'Tis what we do when loved ones die
Approach the coffin over there
One last kiss and say a prayer'
And so I went his box of wood
Being brave, the best I could
Uncertain though about that kiss
She'd asked me place upon dead lips.

Now as I looked upon his face
To tell the truth my heart did race
For his the first I'd ever looked
Dead as dead and twice as much
The deadest man I've ever seen
No one deader's ever been
As staring him did I then blink
Uncle George looked at me and winked

I've never run so fast have I
Since that day George winked his eye
From out the coffin I did stare
It raised the hackles of my hair
I hit my bike at running speed
And rode it like the Devil's steed
And though I was but six or seven
I prayed the Lord lock him in Heaven

And now I am a man I smile
Those mysteries weaned when once a child
Ghosts of mine that make a tale
Once turned a youthful glow to pale
For every soul you meet in life
Can tell a tale most ghostly like
To even now give pause to think
Was it George or Death who winked?

M J Banasko

A GIRL I KNOW

A girl I know
is large and obscene,
with devil eyes
unkempt and unclean.

A huge square jaw,
repugnant to the core,
breath that could
knock a horse to the floor.

An Adam's apple
as big as a pear
and dirty, fungal
facial hair.

A quality aimed to
destroy one's soul,
a belly rotund
as a salad bowl.

A brutal backside
repulsive to an eye,
a voice that would
make a baby cry.

I'm happy to say
she's on the mend
thank God for that!
She's my girlfriend.

Brian Conaghan

THE PRETTIEST PENTIUM PRINCESS IN THE WORLD!

The one I love's such a sweetie,
She really looks so cute -
Yet she knows PCs completely -
My babe is quite astute!
She truly digs the Internet
With e-mails up to here!
Whilst other girlies choose to fret,
She proves a pioneer!
She went to college, learnt a lot
And passed exams as well!
She put the teachers on the spot,
She's got so much to tell!
With static-wristband off she goes!
That modem's going in!
Those useless files come to a close,
Moved to the refuse bin!
Her website gets a million hits!
She's famous, yet still nice!
That's why I love that girl to bits.
It's great that she's so wise!
She's getting richer every day -
She takes me out each night!
Not once has she asked me to pay -
That's perfectly alright!
I'm saving up to buy a ring
To seal our happiness!
Who makes me feel like I'm a King?
My Pentium Princess!

Denis Martindale

No!

There's a lot to be said for a woman in bed
Warm, soft and smooth to the touch
But beware of the moment, the moment you dread
That 'not tonight' knee in the crutch!

Bill Goulden

THE TAIL OF COOKING FAT

(For Cheryl Burton)

Cooking Fat, the cat
caught a big, black rat
wearing a bizarre hat.
Under the hat he kept a bat
with a whack went 'splat'
on the head of poor Cooking Fat.

Still, serves him right
to exercise his might
on something half his height.
But what a fright, he did incite
just the other night
on that poor, rodent mite.

So with a head full of pain
and feelings of disdain
out he went into the rain.
He vowed never again
to hurt or maim
a creature with a different name.

But guess what I heard the other day?
I heard a shrew had got in his way
whilst he was out for a play.
The poor shrew had no time to pray
and on the garden path did lay
. . . for Cooking Fat to splay.

It's a cat's nature and we must not resent
the fact that a cat will be hell bent
on sharing his catch most recent.
Remember though, a cat will not relent
and that the result of his evil time spent
could end up being your present.

Martyn Thompson

BUSY NANNY

Who are these nans
Who watch TV
In this twenty-first
Century?

I swim each day
Travel, no fear
Wet suit, so I
Can swim all year.

I sing and dance,
Belong to clubs.
Use computer and cam
Do video dubs.

I walk the dog
And talk to all
Then clear mud splashes
From the hall.

I visit grand-kiddies
Must be fair!
Return so tired
Sink into chair

Programme starts
Now what is this?
Loo . . . ks qui . . . te goo . . . d
Yaaawwwn, zzz, zzz!

Di Castle

A POEM FOR YOUR LOO

Here you sit,
Feeling, oh so tight,
Red faced
Pushing with all you might!

Stop that!
Read me a-while, relax, be calm,
Place your hands on your tummy,
Come on! Try it!

Keeping your hands in one spot,
Make a circle-like motion.
Think of a warm, sunny day.

Imagine you're lying on the hay,
With nothing to do.
Feel the relaxation of the moment.

Then you're not so red faced,
Nor disgraced
By swear words,
But the pulp of solids has passed,
You're just a little hot assed!

Maria Ann Cahill

ARMY MAJOR

key in door, shouts 'hello'
silence greeted me
sniff sniff sniff
christ wot's that smell
mmmmmmm - very much cat pee
the fruit bowl floats in urine
the bananas have a fur
that filthy feline dirty cat
has a cheek tae purr

like an army major
i go from room to room
swearin' like a bleedin' trooper
those wains best be home soon

the dinin' room resembles
a scene fae sum launderette
piles an' piles o' washin'
that's no been washed, a bet

my bedroom next - before a went
a very strongly said
'don't go in, keep oot it's mine'
but some git's been in ma bed

the bog it smelled of men, ye know that pong ye get!
when boys have peed upon the mat, an' left it soakin' wet
outside in the garden ye canny see the grass
for tops of bloody beer bottles, growin' there amass

the fridge, it houses vodka
and a little else I see
no food, no welcoming dinner
prepared to dad and me.
this army major's waitin'
cos she's now been home a day
her wains are awfully clever
they've had the sense tae stay away
i've done a shop, 'ave cleaned the hoose,
'ave washed the bathroom floor
'ave changed ma beds and polished up
and then 'ave cleaned some more
this army major's waitin'
waitin' behind the door
cos when her bleedin' wains come home
she's gonna knock them to the floor

Jackie Neil

THE BRAIN HAS GONE AWOL!

I left some of my brain in the local PO
Seems to be much the same, wherever I go.
My brain's nearly empty, I've not much to show,
Doctors say it's my age but what do *they* know!

It's nothing like that, it's the pressure of life
And it's sometimes been known to cause trouble and strife.
It's never the husband but always the wife -
Ha! That's what *he* thinks, just beware of my knife!

I must shop for some brains and an energy bag
To help prevent everything starting to sag.
It's beginning to be just a bit of a fag,
I forget what I'm looking for - oh what a drag!

Ah yes! I remember! I want a new brain,
And this energy bag that I'll look for again.
But now good intentions have gone down the drain.
It's far too much trouble *and* it's starting to rain . . .
I give up!

Paddy Jupp

BRITISH SISTER

Sister a Brit
Me a Yank!
Then my heart slowly sank.
Is this a dream? Is mother mad?
'No!' she replied, 'blame your Dad.'

In the Air Force he came to be
Stationed in Norfolk, so happily.
Cold nights produced this child
Though let me assure you, it wasn't mild!

As I asked what was she like?
The response I heard was not to my delight.
'You see my dear, we named her Jayne.'
She screamed all the time, driving neighbours insane
So the Queen had asked us to leave
Her country desperate for a reprieve.

James Milton

THE BLONDE-HAIRED, BLUE-EYED, CHERUB-FACED DICTATOR

Wrapped in a blanket, placed in my arms; the delicate fingers, the beautiful eyes. I succumbed in an instant to his newborn charms. He captured our hearts, invaded our lives, we the subjects, his every whim our command. This blonde-haired, blue-eyed, cherub-faced dictator, who cried out his orders throughout the day and the night.

Covered by a blanket, lying in his cot; parental ears ever alert to his every snuffle, stirring, sneeze and cough; room service, ready to answer his bidden call. In the night-light glow we bow down before him, winding up the music of his monotonous bedtime toy. We're in the hands of a blonde-haired, blue-eyed, cherub-faced dictator who wakes us up early and taxes our sleep.

Kicking off his blanket, sitting in his pram, refusing to sanction the parental sleeping plan. Dodging pedestrians, negotiating kerbs, fiddling with car seats, wrestling with straps, his fold-away carriages I can never collapse; whatever the weather, day or night, for his convenience, we pound the streets. We're the subjects of a blonde-haired, blue-eyed, cherub-faced dictator, whose daily routines regulate our lives.

Pulling back our blanket, playing havoc with our legs; his mastery now complete as he sleeps within our bed. Early every morning, he rapidly deploys his vast army of toys and demands the unconditional surrender of the television controls. Our lives have been invaded by a blonde-haired, blue-eyed, cherub-faced dictator whose currency of compliance is chocolate and sweets.

K J Hooper

BLOOMING CHEEK

We were travelling to France on the ferry,
I had never been on one before.
We wanted to go to the toilet
So we searched all around for the door.
Up and down steps, along gangways we ran,
My sister and I.
I wanted to *go* so badly
I thought I was going to cry.
Then at last we came to the toilet,
We rushed in as fast as we could.
We each went into a cubicle and did,
Well you know, what we should!
On going to the basins to wash
We noticed a man standing there.
He was looking at us in the mirror
While wetting and combing his hair,
He looked very shocked when he saw us
And he made a hasty retreat.
Especially when Sis gave him one of her *looks!*
Whilst exclaiming aloud, 'What a cheek!'
Now what was he doing in the Ladies?
Had he had some evil intent?
We looked back, after making our exit,
The sign on the door it said *Gents.*

N J Stephens

UNTITLED

Some said she was quite a gal,
in fact she was everyone's pal.
Along came a bloke
who was really nodcoke
not knowing she was dasypygal.

It wasn't hard to compute
why men for her were in pursuit,
but when her clothes were removed
displaying her grooves
there was no doubt that she was hirsute!

It wasn't her fault she was hairy
but some found it quite scary.
When she went to bed
by some, it was said,
to caress her, one should be wary!

D R Thomas

PEN AND INK

I like to sit and write some rhymes
I've done it now so many times
All alone, I then compose
A verse or two of rambling prose

Sometimes it can be a tease
Sometimes words just flow with ease
Sometimes good and sometimes worse
Rather like this little verse

I dip the pen into the ink
Scratch my head and have a think
Now what would Wordsworth have to say
If he were sitting here today

And Kipling, Byron, Keats and Blake
Just how long would each one take
To pen their words for all to see
Those splendid lines of poetry?

Then gazing through my window pane
I hear a lark in full refrain
And all across the rolling hills
Are golden fields of daffodils

An idea comes to me at last
The nib is dry, I must work fast
But when I write, it's as I feared
Because the ink has disa . . .

Calvin Clarke

YOU ARE THE BEATLE MAN

I was sitting in a cafe, drinking tea
When a man suddenly approached me.
He said, 'Son, do you know who I am?
I said, 'Sorry mate, I don't understand!'
Then he pointed to a door
There was dust on the floor
I was told of an old dark place
He had a ghostly look on his face.

He asked me to follow him in
It was cold and it smelt like a bin,
There was drip from a tap in the corner
It was an old barber shop and it used to be warmer.
As I turned to leave the place
Suddenly I saw his face
I couldn't believe who I saw -
John Lennon's ghost was standing by the door.
He said, 'Son do you know who I am?'
Nervously I said, 'Yeah, you're that Beatle man!'

So we walked to Mathew Street
He had no shoes on his feet,
A T-shirt and a ripped pair of jeans
All this time I wondered where had he been?
At the Cavern he stopped by the door
I noticed there was no shadow in a puddle on the floor.
He smiled and he waved his hand
I just could not understand.
I had to get to a phone
To tell the operator, John Lennon was home!

Every time I walk past the Cavern,
There's three men standing on the door
Two of them are doormen
The other is John Lennon, that's for sure.

People walk on by
With a cheeky grin and a glint in their eye
The doormen let them in
They walk past Lennon, they cannot see him.

I was sitting in a cafe drinking tea,
When a man suddenly approached me
He said, 'Son, do you know who I am?'
'Of course!' I said, 'I was your biggest fan!'

Stephen A Owen

THE BEST MEDICINE

Take a good size mixing bowl,
Whatever sort will do,
Always make sure laughter first,
Goes in this magic brew!
Add a dose of friendship -
An old recipe for years,
Try not to stir the mixture up
Or there will be some tears!
Fry the badness out the good,
And season with a prayer,
Then dish up a nice, big slice
Of love we can all share!

Kerri Fordham

MILKMAN'S FOLLY

I got up one morning and opened my front door,
expecting my two usual pints but found that there were four.

I left a note for the milkman explaining what he'd done,
I thought that it would put an end of too much milk for one.

I got up next morning and opened my front door,
I wasn't expecting any milk but found he'd left two more.

Hoping he would read it, I left a note that night,
My cat's full up, I've had enough, please understand my plight!

I got up this morning and opened my front door,
I found a carton of double cream, *Oh no!* I thought, not more!

I glanced out of my window, the milkman I did see,
Creeping up my path with pints, one, two and three!

Patricia Coates

MAGIC NUMBERS

The Grand Wizard of Numbers
The greatest wizard of them all
Assembled the wizards in the Great Hall of Camelot
All the wizards bowed to the One, the greatest of them all.

Let there be magic, let there be a pile of gold,
Listen to the Wizard or there'll be no magic in Camelot
Without magic there can be no luck
Never, never in a million or even in a billion
Remember, remember! One is the greatest number of them all.

Adam was lonely all alone, so I took a bone
From the core of his soul. Lady Luck have magic
The numbers multiply
There has to be two in a bed or there will never be more
There has to be a real mountain of gold
Dare you deny the Wizard his share. You will be unlucky
Even for ever more!
Gold is the manure that makes the magic grow
The Grand Wizard of Numbers, claims the crown of Camelot.

Two in a bed on the seventh, the perfect number is seven.
Roll over, roll over, again and again!
Until the jackpot will make a King blush
Instead of small change. The jackpot will be great.
To ransom even the famed King of Camelot.
Remember, remember, One who wears the crown of Numbers
One is the greatest of them all. You have to honour the Wizard.
To try to cheat a Wizard! He will turn you into a herd of pigs, for sure.

In '77 the Wizard wrote to the Grandees of Camelot
A game plan, two in a bed.
The Grandees poo-pooed it, they were riding high
On the crest of the waves.
A super jackpot, 'Obscene!' the Grand Dukes declared.

Imagine a syndicate, here, there, anywhere?
10, 20, 30, 40 or more - the chance of a lifetime.
The dream ticket beyond compare?
They may even have the pleasure in the sun
Then back to the grind, doing their mundane jobs.

Will Richard, the Virgin King
Be crowned the King of Camelot?
Lord knows he may listen to the Wizard.
Maybe, just maybe, he may only be half as arrogant
As the Dukes and Grandees of Camelot?
Mickey Mouse is the king of dreams,
Taking the mickle from one and all.

Lorand Tabith

A POEM A DAY

An apple a day
keeps the doctor away
Some garlic a day
keeps the vampires at bay
A poem a day
keeps the mind at play

Ali Collins

BAKING TIMES

I look at a book of all the recipes
inside I've ever made

Sticky toffee, chocolate cake, honey,
bread that my mam used to bake,
when I sat up in my pram.
Raisin crispies. Iced buns to name but a few
but all those mistakes too!

I hated the cooker, I just wish for once
it would blow a huge fuse,
then I'd nip down the Chinky for a stir-fry.
Stewed apples baked in a pie, too huge
roly pudding, roll out too far to diet.

I may not be Delia Smith
but my cooking isn't a hit or a miss.
I get my rewards when the children sing,
'Home-made sausage rolls, gingerbread and things,
to bake this lot, fit for a king!'

A J Renyard

THE QUEEN OF SHEEBA

I stood up straight to ease my aching back, a short respite
from my toil. Wiping sweat from my brow, I looked up to the
flats above, I noticed a grey haired old lady watching me work.
I smiled and waved to her but drew only a stony glare, obviously
she was not amused by my attentions.

I called her Queen Victoria, she had that look about her, rather prim
and condescending. For days she watched me work without a flicker.

The owner arrived for his weekly inspection, I asked him about the
old lady in the flats above.
'What old lady? I own those flats, they're boarded up,
nobody lives up there and hasn't done for six years.
The flats all need major refurbishment to make them
habitual. Which window exactly does she appear at?'
So I point out the window on the third floor.
'That's the kitchen window, leave this with me,
I'll investigate.'

An hour later the owner returns.
'I've checked out the flats, all locks are in place,
there's nobody at all up there. You must have seen a ghost
young man. I should lay off the whiskey.' Says he with a wink.

As this conversation takes place, over his shoulder I can clearly
see old Victoria at the window again. I spin him around and ask him,
'Well who the hell is that then? The Queen of Sheeba?'
The owner looks up, gulps and calls out, *'Oh Mother!'*

P J Littlefield

ME AND NOG

I've got a super computer,
Not very well known, it's called *'Nog!'*
It's clever and very obedient,
Like a little, extremely well-trained dog.

Here's the sad bit, I'm not very wealthy,
So I have to eat out-of-date food,
Like mushy tomatoes, stale bread, black bananas
And a five year old Tesco Christmas pud.

I'm okay, 'cause my guts are very resilient.
In fact, they must be petrified.
I'm as tough as a chunk of cast iron,
Anyone else would have curled up and died.

With my *Nog*, my friendly computer,
I write my graphics real fast.
They call me The Hot *Nog*-Grapher
And I'll soon make a fortune that's vast.

But for now, I'm just a little impoverished,
With guts, tough as a steel lined boot.
I'm only a hard, poor Nog-Grapher
Of that there is no serious dispute!

Jerome Kiel

THE LAUGHING SAILOR

I watch the fish swim past me
Think of my old life
The sun and you
Little seahorse smiles at me
Thinks I look old at the bottom of the sea.
Once I was fat, like a Cheshire cat
Roses in my cheek,
Big black hat.
On a tall ship I sailed on the sea.
Looking for gold at the
Bottom of the sea.
Till a wave covered me
Now I live at the bottom of the sea.

Helen Owen

LEYLAND ALBION ICE MEN
(Thanks to Kevin and Paul for a good night out!)

Kevin is our manager, his hair is going thin.
Paul is his assistant and always has a grin.
They put their heads together to give the boys a treat
'Lets all go skating, slip-sliding, on your feet!'

So on the motorway to Blackburn, the team set out to drive,
And at 7.30 precisely they all began to arrive.
Kitted out with skates, they wobbled to the ice
Dressed in their winter clobber, they all looked very nice.

Paul was first to hit the ice, his skating was quite good,
Although I think his belly was full of Christmas pud.
Kevin was another tale, as he tottered round the side,
At first I thought he was dancing, demonstrating the Palais Glide.
He spent more time upon his bum his trousers were quite wet,
I think I heard one of the lads say, 'Let's go and get the vet!'

As he gained in confidence he moved into the middle
His pants had now got so wet, he'd had a jimmy riddle.
But all in all he did quite well, he gave us all a laugh,
He needs to stick to football as his skating is quite naff!

Ivor Percival (Spectator)

DREAMER

The other night
I dreamed of
Having a
Wonderful personality
But when I awoke;
I was the same old b*****d!

Alan Holdsworth

CHRISTMAS VISITOR

Gray lies in his bed
Christmas Eve 2101
Waiting for Santa to come
A person in red unlike none

Santa does arrive
In Gray's lonely room
He looks up to see
Santa over him loom

Gray pulls off the red coat
See it is Debs in disguise
Beds Debs and makes magic
Love so hot it fries

H G Griffiths

Up The Wall

For all of my life I have suffered,
    all sorts of horrible pains,
I've had every complaint you can mention,
    from acne to varicose veins.

So if any young medical student
    who a general practitioner would be,
If you find it tough out there - don't despair,
    you can come and practice on me.

F R Smith

ICY WATER

Plunging in the water, oh my God I cried,
Icy water engulfs my head,
Freezing cold, chattery teeth,
No one here, help! I cried.
Cannot breathe, seatbelt's stuck,
I am finished, fading fast,
Unconscious now, soon be gone,
Going, going, is this the end?
Dreaming of beautiful faces
With perfect features,
Waking up in hospital asking
Questions. How? How? How?

Terry Ramanouski

PUBS

The bright lights
The macho-man
   Draw us
To this land

Bars and stools
And people too
   Pint too
In their hands

Weird and strange
This macho-land
   Faces blurry
This dreary band

Herd of cattle
A watering flock
   Lips apart
Drunk the lot.

Ray Rapson

CAT-O'-NINE-TAILS

I remember well this neighbour
  whose husband ate cat food
I kept telling her this would poison him
  but my advice did her no good

She said he had taken it for years
  and it had never did him harm
So what I said didn't frighten her
  nor cause her much alarm

I told her that all the cat food
  wasn't made for the humans plate
But still she kept on serving him
  being rather obstinate

Then one day as I returned from work
  I saw a funeral at her house
I then approached her for to ask
  if this happened to be her spouse

She said it was, and would like to let me know
  that poison was not defined
As it was found he had a broken neck
  through licking at his behind

Lachlan Taylor

PICKLED EGGS AND MUSHY PEAS

Pickled eggs and mushy peas,
That's what I had for my tea,
Then to the girlfriend's, dressed up smart to meet the parents,
Welcomed in through the door, my stomach rumbles, I must not fart.
'Cup of tea,' her mother said to me,
'Slice of cake,' but this I know my guts won't take,
Something now on its way,
I need the toilet without delay,
But still I sit to be polite and make a good impression,
Cheeks are clenched.
'Where's the loo?' I said out loud, 'I just can't wait!'
'Up the stairs on the left!'
I make a dash,
I'm on the pot, I make a splash,
With relief I rid the poo!
But now the stench. The pong of gas,
I spray the air hoping it will disguise the smell,
Brave face on I descend the stairs.
Mother and Father looking puzzled,
Now things are silent,
Awkwardness in the air,
Now her mother goes upstairs,
I hear a scream of disgust,
That was the end of my affair.
Pickled eggs and mushy peas,
I recommend you be aware
Or with a girl you just won't fare!

Daren Armstrong

Words Elusive

Crossword puzzles can be such a passion
that the time I give I have to ration
so that floors get swept and the washing done.
These chores, however, are not much fun,
so back I creep to wrestle again,
just one more time, now what is that name?
Oh, bother, oh bother, it's another fault!
Something, something B, blank and then a 'T'.
I rack my brains, what can it be?
A knock at the door, can I smell gas?
The saucepan's boiled dry, alas, alas!
The phone starts ringing, time is moving on,
If I knew the answer, I'd sing a little song
but it's not going to happen, my luck is out today,
must wait until tomorrow before I once again can play.

Daphne McFadyen

DISPATCHES

I fell off my nicotine patch . . .
. . . It wasn't a good match!
After thirty years I might have known
There'd to a catch! . . .
. . . Like it wouldn't stick!
It to me or me to it,
It doesn't matter now
Not a whit!
The relationship's too strong
And I can't get away . . .
. . . It doesn't matter what you say.
And yes, I know tomorrow's another day,
But this day I'm off my nicotine patch
Like the opposite sex, not a good match!

Katie Norton

MRS BLOOMER'S BLOOMERS

They were torn and they were tattered,
At t'backside they were shattered,
    For *'er* backside was too big for 'em, y'see,
And no matter 'ow she tried
She could never get inside
    Without a mighty 'eave above t'knee!

There was lace around t'legs
That got tangled in t'pegs
    When she 'ung 'em on t'line outside to dry,
So instead o' dainty threads
They were 'angin' down in shreds,
    Ee, they were a pretty sight to meet t'eye!

Now, t'colour it were red,
And she really should be dead
    For a bull once charged Ma Bloomer from be'ind,
When 'er rear end 'e espied
To toss 'er 'igh 'e tried,
    Now that poor old bull must surely be 'alf blind!

Ee, by gum, you should 'ave seen 'er!
Not an athlete could be keener
    Than Ma Bloomer as she raced right up t'field!
Wi'er bloomers slippin' longer
And 'er shrieking growin' stronger
    Ee, it surely would 'ave made your senses reel!

Now they're worse than torn and tattered
For they're completely shattered!
    Not a shred o' lace is left around t'knee,
Now I 'ear she goes wi'out 'em!
But I don't know owt about 'em,
    For that's a sight I wouldn't want to see!

Betty McIlroy

DAD IN FRONT OF THE TELLY

Dad in front of the telly,
Is that a surprise to you or me?
He sits with his eyes glued to the box,
In his slippers and woollen socks.
If it's football, you know the score,
If you're trying to sleep, he'll shout, *'That's four!'*
You don't need a commentator with my dad,
He talks to himself, (and he thinks I'm mad)!
When it comes to films, he knows the plot,
The good, the bad, he's seen the lot.
Clint Eastwood is his favourite part,
And knows his lines off by heart.
'Go ahead, make my day.'
I wish he'd make mine and go away.
Then there's comedies, where he laughs and laughs again,
It's a right carry-on, like a kid in his playpen.
Time and energy he does devote,
To the worn out buttons on the control remote.
Yet he will pause at the intermission,
And like James Bond has made his decision.
'Put the kettle on, make the tea.'
As you've guessed, that's down to Mum or me.
'Two sugars,' I say. 'Shaken not stirred.'
'Don't be silly,' he says. 'That was Bond that you heard.'
Mum does get a chance to watch her East-End soap,
While Dad does the crossword until he can't cope.
When he has finished, it's back to the screen,
So's Mum with her knitting, of which she is keen,
And I, at my paper, penning the rhymes,
Our family's content, with chosen pastimes.

Christopher W Wolfe

IF ONLY TOWELS COULD TALK...

After I had showered one day
I reached for a towel as one might,
I dried all my parts, and the bits in between,
Then I straightened up with a fright.

For what came into my mind just then
Was a revelation you'll agree,
'If only towels could talk,' was my thought,
What would they say to me?

'Don't be so rough with me if you please,
I'm soft and sensitive and fluffy,
And if you stick me again where you stuck me just then,
I'm likely to get quite huffy!

I deserve a bit more respect I think,
Hanging round and ready to serve,
Going boldly where others would fear to tread -
In fact I think you've got quite a nerve!

When we've done our job, we're tossed aside,
In the washing basket we go,
Amongst the discarded underwear,
It's not very pleasant you know.

Then, it's into the washing machine,
An extra hot wash we suffer,
We're spun around 'til we feel quite sick,
Then conditioned with built-in fluffer!

So next time you use us, spare us a thought,
Don't' take us for granted no more,
Because come the towel revolution,
We might just tell all that we saw!

Janina Glowala

183

DEAR MILLS AND BOON

Just because their mothers were,
Women don't have to be wimps -
Prisoners of old conventions.
Sex is fellows' force 'majeure'
On emotion, they will skimp -
Loyalty's like school detentions.

For some years now, the fearful
Innocent look on a girl's face
In men's sight, has been a bygone.
Yours books' readers aren't so tearful
Or impeded by irksome grace.
These days, Jane's as bold as John.

Praise your authors, please, for taking
Us to be loved in exotic
Climes where winter is taboo.
None of us would dislike waking
Up hurt, (when life's gone psychotic) -
To see Dr Feverfew.

Gillian Fisher

WHAT A CAPER

He flew in a balloon
With a silver spoon,
Over the Atlantic
He got a bit frantic.

When he arrived at the gates
Of the United States,
It was quite a caper
As he 'landed' on a skyscraper.

The firemen helped his descent
And charged not a cent.
So he gave them the spoon
And wished them 'Good afternoon!'

He appeared on TV
And said, 'Fiddle dee dee
What's all the fuss?'
So he jumped on a bus.

He alighted at Boston
Where he met Flossie Watson.
He stayed for the rest of his life
And wrote postcards to his wife!

J T Purdom

FATHER CHRISTMAS

Father Christmas came to town travelling on his sleigh,
But one reindeer almost went on strike when they were on their way.
'The sleigh is very heavy and I'm dropping to my knees,
Just trying to cope with everything, and trying hard to please.
I'll call in health and safety for old Christmas is too fat,
With everyone too greedy, and Christmas up there sat.
Oh Santa you've been eating too many cakes and pies,
And your bottom barely fits up there with your extra bulbous thighs.
You'll have to cut your food down or I'll sit, and not move on,
I may be big and beefy but I'm not that blessed strong.'
So health and safety came in time to save our Christmas Day,
It wasn't very long you know when they were on their way.
They sent in Santa's fairy with a tiny magic wand,
And old Santa and the fairy began to grow a bond.
He said, 'Sit up here my beauty, right here upon my knee,
And wave that tiny magic wand, then Rudolf will let me be.'
So the fairy feeling very shy she sat on Santa's knee,
Her blushes very obvious when Santa gave a squeeze.
He said, 'Oh fairy you are beautiful, I am in love with you,
Can you get rid of all this weight, make me a man so new?'
So the fairy feeling very warm had made a special wish,
Because she thought that Santa was a very moreish dish.
The weight just fell off Santa but the fairy grew in size,
It was just around the middle where she wore her new disguise.
For the fairy made a special wish that would make old Santa blush,
And the blood came gushing to his face in quickened flowing rush.
The fairy flew off quickly but she barely left the ground,
For the bump around her middle had grown so big she'd found.
For old Santa had his Christmas gift whilst she sat upon his knee,
Next Christmas you will find my friends, two fairies on the tree.
The one will look so very cute with a tutu made in white,
But the other will be dressed in red with a nose that's big and bright.

Wendy Evans

ON THE TOWN

Two ladies went to town,
Sales on with all prices down,
Bargain hunting was the game,
No two floors sold the same.

Dresses and shoes first on the list,
Appetite satisfied met their thirst.
Credit cards were all the rage,
Money locked up in a golden cage.

Next level the haberdashery store,
Big reductions who can ask for more?
Food hall enticing tastebuds recall,
Fourth floor beckoning to toylands mall.

Santa's grotto many children around,
The place young dreams can be found.
Big and hearty a great beaming smile,
White beard and whiskers a magic style.

Christmas spirit was in the air,
Father Christmas with pleasures to share.
The ladies having a wonderful time,
Money no object spending sublime.

Intoxicated the sales made their day,
Santa Claus is coming on his sleigh.
Would you marry him? He's such a dear
Oh no! He 'comes' only once a year!

Norman S Brittain

BLOODY GNATS

The bloody gnats are biting
I don't know why it is
They find me so inviting
But that's just how it is

I don't mind just a little nip
That's really quite OK
But bite a leg off to the hip
Is rather a lot to pay

They really had a go at me
Great bites blue and red
One bit me just below the knee
It sent me off me head

This time he's got me on the thigh
It's come up red and fat
It's really quite embarrassing
To show somebody that

I won't go out tomorrow
You don't know what's to come
He might be out there waiting
To bite me on the bum!

Pauline A E Marshall

THE MEANING OF CHRISTMAS

The excitement is starting,
Showing upon the faces,
Christmas lights are flashing,
Children asking for the latest crazes.

What will it be this year,
Board games, bats and balls?
Or something really special,
Like a scooter from Uncle Paul?

Thoughts of fun and presents,
Laughter and tears too,
They are all so very natural,
Yet it's not all - about me and you.

Christmas is a special time,
But would not even be,
If it weren't for the birth of Baby Jesus,
In a land far across the sea.

Cheryl Campbell

RHYME AND REASON

I make no apology, (though back in mythology)
Poems were written in rhyme,
I'm just the same, but no claim to fame;
It drifts through my mind; so I rhyme every time.

Rhymes are in my blood; so it isn't any good
People trying to alter this stance.
I shall not alter; not even falter
On narrative, there at a glance.

So don't let us judge, (the two camps won't budge)
Get on with whatever you choose.
If it attracts, then please don't attack
The authors who enjoy writing prose.

Ivy Cawood

ODE TO DRINKING

Time to get going, time to party hard,
jump in the car, that's parked in the yard.
You wonder how it got there, oh hell, who cares?
Another night of drinking, more cabs to pay fares.

Entering the bar, your friends all around,
shooting shot after shot, swigging the beers down.
Time's getting late, hunger pains you feel,
you think to yourself, *hmmmmmm*, pizza's the deal.

Pepperoni, sausage, mushrooms, onions, oh yeah! Oh yummy,
anchovies, *oh hell no*, get that crap off, damn where's the money?
The smell whiffs up, right up your nose, mouth-watering, drooling,
another shot or two, *oh no* the cheese is cooling.

Stumble through the door you go, *oops* the pizza's on the floor,
oh well never mind, pick it back up, damn forgot to shut the door.
Crawling to the bed, *oh no*, the room's in a twirl,
somebody *please* help me, I'm gonna hurl.

Nikohl Medley

MODERN TIMES?

I remember the day my father said, 'Now listen to me my son,
I know that this may be a shock, but really I'm your mum.'

'My mother,' I said slowly - 'Oh dear, how very sad.
Well if my father is my mother - then my mum must be my dad
And my aunt must be my uncle - and vice versa too
In that case Mum.' I said to *him* - 'I have some news for you.

If my mother is my father - my dad my mother too,
You know you thought you had a son
Well sadly that's not true!

There's somethin' I have to tell you
I feel that it's time I oughta . . .
You call me Son, you think I'm male,
Well really . . . I'm your daughter!'

David Mark Evans

SHOPPING AT MARKS

There's a place that keeps our family
Richly fed and finely dressed
Although the cost when viewed annually
May be higher than the rest
The superior store that's coloured green
I think you know the one I mean!

They say it's better quality
So satisfaction's guaranteed
There's surely no frivolity
When meeting my wife's discerning need
For wild horses could not wrench her
From between the aisles of Marks & Spencer.

A celestial force is clearly focused
Near the chicken sweet and sour
Which draws my family in like locusts
Tray loads eaten by the hour
For cooking turns so very hard
When you're poised and ready with a charge card.

And then to clothes, a new domain
Whether browsing or the sales
It's hard for me to ascertain
The magnetism of those rails
I can only stand and stare
As they empty childrenswear.

And so a warning from this writer
To shoppers striving perfect peace
Because the milk is visibly whiter
Our excursions are unlikely to cease
But beware if sales are reported to rocket
Cos we've got the receipt and we're likely to swap it!

Stephen Morley

RULES FOR AN UNRULY VIRGIN

If the bachelor vicar invites you to tea,
> Flee.
And the artist wants you to be his new model,
> Toddle.
If a pilot offers you pie-in-the-sky,
> Fly.
So the actor ardently woos you after the show,
> Go.
The computer buff calls you to suddenly text it,
> Exit.
When the suave cowboy builder wants you in his noose,
> Vamoose.
And the boxing instructor thinks you're quite a hit,
> Quit.
If the bed salesman acts like an enormous hunk,
> Bunk.
And the road-runner wants you to be his new bint,
> Sprint.
When the astronaut wants to show you his shuttle,
> Scuttle.
If anyone offers your love life to heat it,
> Beat it.

Jack Scrafton

HOSPITAL HYSTERIA

With great precision
He makes the incision.
Listening to Chopin, Handel and Bach
He'll soon sew up the paunchy stomach.
Peering and leering at the nurses tits
He continues removing his patient's bits.
Eighth operation today
How much longer must he stay?
Very soon he'll be home to his dinner
Is the NHS the winner?

Sacha Cheraton

ON RECEIVING MY WATER BILL
(Ode to the Water Board)

The only water that flows free
Are the tears from my eyes,
Your bill it shocked me just to see
It came as a surprise.

For bath and lav' and washing up,
Your water's used for that,
For cooking and tea in a cup,
But I live in a flat.

No garden hose do I use,
No cars to wash or clean,
I'll not but I'd like to refuse
To up my rate one bean.

The rates are high, it makes me sad,
So I will now be frank,
To pay myself, it's just too bad,
So I'll instruct the bank.

Suzanne Joy Golding

FACTS OF LIFE

My nephew asked his mummy,
How he got into her tummy,
He said, 'Did you swallow me?
Is that how I came to be?
You must have been so hungry,
Instead of one you ate three,
Two brothers and then me.'
As they are triplets you see,
What could his mummy say?
Aaron was not going away,
Without his answer that day.

Mummy said, 'I had you three
As you are so nice you see,
Nicer sons could not be.'
Then his mummy said to me,
'What do you think Auntie She?'
With Mummy I had to agree,
I understood why she had three,
A prouder auntie could not be,
My nephews, are very special to me,
Greg, Aaron and Ross, all three.

Sheila Walters

THE ALARM CLOCK

When I hear that sound, so loud and shrill,
I crawl out of bed against my will.
I run the bath - the water's cold,
The kids had got there first I'm told!

Breakfast is over - toast all gone,
And someone's left the cooker on.
They always keep me on the hop,
And all I hear is 'celebrity pop'!

I'm off to work for some peace and quiet,
But instead of that, there's a bit of a riot!
Someone's pinched the petty cash -
And the office has taken a bit of a bash.

After a long and tiring day
It's time to drive my car away -
Car won't start, then my heart sank -
There was no petrol in the tank!

I planned to have a quiet night,
Not a party, with a bit of a fight.
When at last I crawled to bed,
Whispering to myself, I said,
'I won't hear that sound, so loud and shrill,'
I've put it on *their* window sill!

Milly Hatcher

MURDER ON THE DANCE FLOOR

I will never, ever dance again,
Why? To save feet, I refrain,
The example I give on the pain I deliver,
Is a double date I was on in Colchester,
Me, my mate, his girl and her friend,
One nice and warm, May weekend,
Nice drink and meal out,
Then onto a nightclub was the shout,
Things were well, after we had something to eat,
Now for the reason I stay in my seat,
Nightclub: 70s disco night,
No sign of, to be, the eventual plight,
In, no problem, everything nicely under way,
DJ puts on a slow song, I move in to make my play,
Doh! I've just stepped onto her foot,
She winces in discomfort,
I move away, so as to relieve the pain,
Oh no! I've done it again,
Everyone's looking at me,
As she writhed on the floor in agony,
On come the lights, they turn off the din,
Open the fire escape doors to let the ambulance men in,
She was one of the loveliest people you could meet,
But I ended up breaking bones, in both her feet,
So if you see me in a bar, function or dance hall,
Don't ask me to dance, if you value each metatarsal.

Mark Redfern

I'M FREE

I'm free; I've lost those chains that fettered me!
Free of work and hectic pace, at last I've found a better place
No nine to five - *that* boring job - now it's time to come alive!

Sure - there's wrinkles round my eyes and my chin has found its twin
The bosom, once firm and neat, is slowly slipping to my feet
At last - no need to impress - I'm free to choose the way I dress.

Not for me, a nip and tuck - I really can't believe my luck!
The alarm is going in the bin - no need to wake up to that din
So what has set my heart on fire - the time has come to retire!

Ros Heller

LAUGHTER, MIRTH

Laughter it's said, helps medicine go down.
Recently in a surgical ward
Mirth, very little heard
Patients' times past, slow to recall
Many a waiting life of here-after.

Carers for infirm, elderly
Angels without wings
Sharing duties
Ease of pain
Comforts for all, to bring.

Late, last night there commotion heard
Sounds of cock-doodle do!
Extra nurses rushed in ward
Looked under beds all
No sight, sounds of lovebirds there.

I heard a patient (coming out of anaesthesia)
Say, is it Christmas time?
Another said,
Are there eggs
For breakfast menu, mine?

'Twas a blind lady's talking watch
Giving correct night-time
Laughter filled the ward.
Giggles too, all night through
Helping medicine go down, it was certainly proved.

Ivy Lott

FRIENDS

If you think you'd like a friend
    But don't know what to do,
Please don't be downhearted
    This poem's just for you,
Now here's a little secret
    It's my philosophy,
And you can try it for yourself,
    I know it works for me,
Be kind to people that you meet
    And greet them with a smile,
And always stop and say hello
    For just a little while,
And if you do this every day
    Your friends will multiply,
Don't say it wouldn't work for you,
    I know it would, just try,
It's really not so hard to do,
    There's people everywhere,
Just show a little kindness
    And let them know you care,
Just try it now, you'll be surprised
    At all the friends you'll meet,
You might meet someone on a bus
    Or walking in the street,
Some day you'll meet a special friend,
    Someone just right for you,
And perhaps you'll fall in love
    The way that others do,
And all of this can happen
    If you just take this advice,
Just greet a stranger with a smile
    You might meet someone nice.

James Stanley

BREASTFEEDING

But nobody ever complained before,
No one told me at all -
Not my mother, not my husband, no one.
But now this midwife declares
I have flat nipples!

Okay so they don't stick out like film stars do,
Like cherries on iced buns,
Leaping erect to attention,
But that's not normal, surely?
Just a Hollywood invention.

She tries to comfort me in that normal women look silly when it's cold
As their nipples show through their clothes.
Well, what a hardship;
I can't breastfeed my baby
Because he can't latch on to flat nipples.

There is a possible solution, or two.
You use breast shields, or suction pumps
Or some other hideous contraption.
But no matter of poking or prodding or squeezing
Does anything to solve this problem.

So baby, listen very carefully,
Because I'm doing this just for you,
I'm pumping all my milk into bottles, and then I'm going to sleep,
And when you cry, Daddy will get up and bottle-feed it to you.
Oh what a blessing - flat nipples!

Paula Holt

MY TOM CAT

My head is done in,
The tom cat can't wait to come in.

The next door tom cat thinks
he's a cockerel, he says that
our she-cat is always willing
It's shame she's just come in.

The dog has got his legs crossed
he can't find a tree, he's dying for a p-e-e.

My wife thinks I've got too many
jeans in my genes, as she ties me
to our bed.

Then she tells me she wished that,
I'd be just like that next door's tom cat
but she just like our she-cat
is always willing.

Then she smiles as she tells
me, 'Love you filled
the pram six times so far!'

Paul Wilcox

PREVENTIVE MEDICINE

Dentist, dentist do beware,
It's time for my check-up I do declare,
I'll try not to screech or holler with fright,
Or quake at the knees when the drill comes in sight.

I know I shouldn't be quite so phobic,
I'd much rather be in a class of aerobics,
But every time 6 months comes round
My imagination seems to know no bounds.

I should of noted what was said,
Brush your teeth after you've been fed,
Instead to my dismay I see,
Another filling to pay a fee.

Now the bathroom shelf beholds,
All things I have been told.
Mouthwash, floss and a special toothbrush,
And don't eat sweets or drink strawberry crush!

Nicola Varmen

WHY?

Why do men shake their willies
When to the toilet go?
Why they can't just use paper
I really do not know.

They splash around the toilet seat
And on the floor around their feet
And sometimes they can't aim at all
And it all ends up on the wall.

When man was made, although it was
An engineering feat,
God really should have made him
To sit on a toilet seat

And use a bit of paper
Just like us women do
To dab up all the dribbles
And not leave for us to do.

Kathleen South

THE CHEESE AND TOMATO SANDWICH

The cheese and tomato sandwich was such a laugh,
It made me look really daft.
Tomatoes were wedged in my gums,
And all the juice did run.
My teeth could not bare the strain.
I was struck dumb like one slain.
The cheese melted on my tongue,
And there was more to come.
Who would think while out for a stroll,
The sandwich would take such a heavy toll!

I T Hoggan

MY CHEESY SMILE

I once smiled at my neighbour when he drove out of his driveway,
Then he bashed into another car and I said, 'Have a nice day!'

I once smiled at the milkman, he captured my smile,
Then he dropped a tray of milk when he said he saw it from
                                                    half a mile!

I once smiled at the post lady, when she posted my bills,
She smiled back in an odd way,
Bet she was thinking, I must have taken some funny pills!

I flashed a smile at my then-boyfriend, what a powerful smile I possess,
Because we are now married with children,
It goes to show how a smile can change the day and bring happiness!

Just a little smile brightens up your day,
Even everyone else's as a matter of fact.
So smile now, please do not delay!

Angela Tsang

SUPERHERO

I'm a superhero
and I really am quite good.
Every day I'm out there
fighting crime in my neighbourhood.
The bad guys they all fear me,
they always run and hide.
But they're no match for me,
I've got justice on my side.
I have a cape. It's really cool,
and a mask to hide my face.
I also used to have some gloves
but I lost that pair someplace.
This week I'm on the trail
of the shady Mr Big.
He's going all around our town
in dark glasses and a wig!
But he can't get away from me,
I've seen through his disguise.
Oh, did I happen to mention
that I've got X-ray eyes?
I really should go catch him
but I'm kinda in a fix,
my mum's throwing a party,
'cause today I'm turning six.

M M Graham

WELL WELL!

There once was a lady name Joyce,
Who thought she could ride a white horse
Without any stirrups,
She mounted the horse,
Then fell off again
Of course.

A lady whose name was Mary
Dreamt she could fly like a fairy,
She flew off at midnight
Flapping those delicate wings
Woke herself up in the morning
Snoring.

Wendy Dawson

LOVER'S REQUEST

Let not your skin be like orange peel
Or your face like a spotted dick.
Do not have gardener's fingernails
Or housemaid's knees.
May not your boobs be like fried eggs
Or your bum all fat and flabby.
And the only spare tyre you own
Be on your soft-top BMW.

Moira Clelland

A Poem Of Thwarted Love

Consignia, oh my Consignia why have you gone?
We spent so much to get you,
What have we done wrong?
Sometimes you came in the morning,
Sometimes not at all,
Which was such a shame!
But I fell in love with Consignia,
Especially with your tantalising name,
So curious! Mysterious! Fascinating! Intriguing! Exciting!
Captivating!
But oh Consignia, now you have gone,
Tell me Consignia,
Please Consignia,
What did I do wrong?
Now you have left me!
Deserted me! Cheerless! Lonely and cold!
And now we are back to 'our old love again',
Who for you we pensioned off! Disowned!
Yet he was so reliable! So regular! So kind!
Now he's back with us again
Yes! Our own, dear friend is back again!
Yes 'Royal Mail' is here again!
But tell me Consignia my darling!
Why did he have to go?

Please be happy for us, please!

Leslie Loader

LITTLE WILLIE

Little Willie is such a pest,
putting worms down his vest.
chasing his sister with dead bugs,
too quick to grab to clip round the lug.

Little Willie, the psycho boy,
played with his cat like a toy.
Loving to set fire to his tail,
see it burn and hear him wail.

Little Willie, Satan's child,
makes himself sick to see his bile.
Eating snails and dissecting worms,
plotting trouble and breeding germs.

Little Willie eyes so blue,
what on earth can we do?
He's in the cellar and we've locked the door,
we will let him out when he's 24!

Nicola Pitchers

WHAT'S UP DOC?

I'm sat in your waiting room Doctor,
Your receptionist's terribly kind,
But how can I bring myself Doctor
To tell you just what's on my mind?

He's gone the big navvy with shingles,
A light starts to flash overhead,
'Next patient to see Dr Riley,'
Oh crikey, I wish I were dead!

Dr Riley's a marvellous fellow,
He treated my gran and my mum,
And I wanted to tell him about it
But believe me the words wouldn't come.

'Are you having the runs?' said the Doctor,
'Or dire constipation instead?
Lots of people have piles in the summer,'
I winced but kept shaking my head.

'Are you having delusions of grandeur?
Are you down in dumps, feeling low?
Just nod if I get any warmer,
Halitosis, or mumps, or BO?

Do you have a large boil that is hidden?
Don't tell me - you're wetting the bed?
Or flatulence during the sermon?
Or your pencil is losing its lead?'

'At last,' I cried, 'Doctor, I'll tell you
To save all this trouble and strife,
Oh Doctor - I'm happy and healthy,
Is that *normal* at my time of life?'

Peter Davies

THE WRONG HOUSE

He died in his bed
As he wanted, he said,
Didn't have any family or wife,
Lived at number two
For 80 odd years
Which meant for most of his life.
They went to his house
To measure him up,
Rigor mortis began to set in,
Curled up in a ball
He was facing the wall
With his knees right up to his chin!
So out came the hammer
To straighten him up
As they rolled him on his back
They went for his knees
Looking like mushy peas
After giving him such a good whack!
The poor beggar screamed
As he fell off his bed
And in agony rolled on the floor,
'Ooh ya bugger,' they said,
'We're at the wrong house
We should be at number four!'

Elaine Kelly

LAUGH

To laugh at oneself, is a pleasure we need,
Before the years creep on and we go to seed.
Life's many surprises, good, unlucky, or unfair
Offer the scope we all need, to begin to share.

Laugh and the world laughs with you,
Cry and you cry alone they say,
So away with thoughts of depression and sorrow,
Be ready to show the world, and laugh tomorrow.

To wake in the morning and hear the birds sing,
To look to the sky, for signs of spring,
A beautiful day, to laugh and sing,
Thanks to the Lord, we can enjoy a fling.

So smile and nod, to passers-by now,
Forgetting the furrowed brow of old.
To laugh and joke with comrades, be bold
Show them, a change for the better, you're sold.

C King

HUMOUR

Everything passes with time
The bad, the good, the sublime
I swallowed a ruby
That quickly passed through me
Yes, everything passes with time.

Dawn Sansum

SPANISH JOE

Goodbye Joe
you gotta go
so goodbye-o.

Me don't think
me wanna play
silly old bingo -

Shouts Spanish Joe
me wanna go
so come with me-o.

No - no - no!
Don't wanna go
to silly old bingo -

Don't be mean
I ain't gotta bean
I wanna go-o.

We might win
have some luck
at the bingo -

Your head is thick
it's just a trick
is this bingo -

So stay at home
and have some pie
with mamma-mio!

Mary Skelton

SLIM

(For Matthew)

Slim pulled out his skateboard
He'd hidden it in his bag
Smuggled safely into school
The day began to drag.

He wanted to try his heel flip
But English had got in his way
'Your education is far more important,'
He could hear his mother say.

I'm desperate to do a nine hundred M
A run, a skid or a melon
But last time I went on the half pipe
Wasn't just my kneels I fell on!

Why do I need to read
And it's just crazy learning to write
When I can go to the skatepark
Jumping the kerbs till it's night.

Slim was not really naughty
But he loved just having a laugh
He never meant to knock over Granny
As he did a run on the path.

Slim's thoughts they kept on wandering
As Shakespeare was thoroughly explained
Yeah right just imagine him skating
And Slim started sniggering again.

The teacher was just not amused
'You're cheeky, disruptive and naughty.'
Slim's mates all started to cheer
'You think that sir coz you're 40!'

Susan Stark

DRIVEN MAD

I am a very quiet lady and small
Although people tell me that's not all.
I can if driven, gradually up the wall
Get quite mad, almost explode
With things like noise, a busy road,
People talking loud in a street,
Shouting at children who you would not wish to meet,
One of the loudest noises that does annoy me,
Is when I occasionally watch TV,
Maybe a film, preferably a classic
But the worst thing of all
While absorbed in the film
Comes an advert loud and horrific.
These present days and nights seem filled with noise
And flashing lights!
Music blaring out from cars,
People drunk falling out from bars,
Singing loud along the road they wander
Home, rocking and rolling,
Shouting and singing.
Trying to sleep
My ears are ringing,
You see, my nights are long,
I sleep very little, hardly at all,
So the thing I hate is *noise* it drives me up the wall.

B Clark

UNTITLED
(Sung to the tune of Daisy, Daisy)

Pastry, pastry,
Mix it up in a bowl,
Cut it, shape it,
Or use completely whole.
Fill it with jam or savoury,
Meat with spices and gravy,
It won't last long,
Soon will be gone,
When everyone comes for tea.

E M Gough

MISS MARY DUST MITE

Miss Mary Dust Mite
Lives in a box,
Which she shares with
Miss Poppy,
Her pet fox.

The box
A large market crate.
Marked on its side
In red letters,
Express banner freight.

Miss Mary Dust Mite
Rode to school
On her yellow bike,
Taking with her
Miss Poppy Fox.

In her pyjamas
Which Mary called
Banners,
Her teacher,
Miss Oily Stock, had a fright.

She did not like,
Not a lot,
Seeing,
In red pyjamas
A wild fox
And pretty Mary Dust Mite.

B G Clarke

MECCA MAN

I wish they'd make a robot, to do what I command
It would have to be a male one looking very grand,
Made to obey orders and to grant my every wish
And when I'm feeling hungry, could cook a lovely dish.

Also it would realise, it does not work for pay,
Just to work to please me, my wishes to convey.
To be able to converse with me, please my every whim
And if it made me happy, then would it be a sin?

I could name it what I want, maybe Mecca Man!
I wouldn't take advantage, if it met with all I'd plan!
Mecca could do cooking, washing and housework too
And when it said, I'm finished; I'd find it more to do.

It would help me with computing, especially in a crash,
Tell me all the answers, and how to make some cash.
Then when I'm feeling tired, and desirous of my bed.
Mecca could play music, and stroke my weary head.

One thing about my Mecca man, it never need grow old,
All parts would be renewable, and have a heart of gold.
Then when I die and leave it, I could leave it in my will
To help some other person, their wishes to fulfil.

Joan Prentice

BURNT OFFERINGS

So you're cooking again,
More burnt offerings I see,
You offer me this charcoal,
Why can't you just let me be?
You burn everything that you cook,
You just haven't got a clue,
Why don't you let me do it?
I could do better than you,
You burn the toast
And you burn the beans,
You even burn water
So it seems.

Chris T Barber

THE BALLAD OF NELLY MCPHAIL

I tell you a tale of Nelly McPhail,
Who wound up a whale, and lonely in jail!
When she was a teen, she was a true queen,
The best ever seen, all the girls were so green.

Now it just happened by, she met a cute guy,
Who so made her sigh she'd love till she'd die.
Now that wasn't so, for his love didn't grow,
When the cancer made show, he'd forever glow.

So she laid him to rest, with a hole in her chest,
She'd just lost the best, so she went on a quest.
She'd live life on the pull, not one moment be dull,
She'd brighten the lull, till her heart became full.

Many years passed away, from that lonely cold day,
And she'd not seen the grey, for she still liked to play.
Well one day unaware, she met a boy fair,
With her true love's gold hair, their future they'd share.

Well each moment was bliss, for the lad and his miss,
From their very first kiss, but one problem was this.
Well the problem was age, which caused folk such rage,
They'd made the front page, the old hag and her Paige

So Nelly McPhail wound up in jail,
'Cause the years on the ale had made her look stale.
Who'd look at him now, with the ugly old sow?
Then a thought came somehow I was drugged by the cow.

So to save his poor face, he brought her disgrace,
Though he! Put up chase, she was out of the race.
So in prison she cried, and so lonely she died,
Because he had lied, and to love twice she'd tried.

Sid 'de'Knees

225

BEER AND CRISPS

Because we hate such things as Brahms and Liszt,
And drink our lager, beer and consume crisps,
This does not mean we men are not artists,
The drinking kind, in pubs, if you insist.

We gladly carry on the tradition,
From fathers who beat the prohibition,
Artists, who drank and drank, no exception,
Their beer until their final redemption.

My mates and me are proud of special skills,
We drink all the varieties, brewed real ales,
Some precautions if drinking makes you ill,
Acquired a brand new skill by learning Braille.

But now and then we're getting Brahms and Liszt,
If you can read and follow through my drift,
From drinking beer and consuming our crisps,
We know we're true artists, if you insist.

David M Walford

VITAMINS

All vitamins are good for us,
A, B, C, D and E.

Vitamin A is found in carrots
And they say it helps you see.

Vitamin B is found in cereals
To get you through the day,
And to help release energy
In every possible way!

Vitamin C is the important one,
It helps stop colds and flu,
But too much will make you ill
And too little can cause scurvy too.

Vitamin D can be from the sun,
So to get this vitamin
Is easy for some!

Vitamin E helps skin to breathe
And is an anti-oxidant too,
We all need a mixture of these
And of course,
So do you!

Julia McAllister

THE ROOTS OF ALL EVIL

When molars creak and eye-teeth groan,
It's not a pleasant sound;
When I with toothache whinge and moan,
I'm to the dentist bound.

But when the dentist probes and pries,
It's hard to take what comes,
When what he says is, 'With no lies,
The trouble is your gums!

You'll have to have some teeth removed,
I'm sorry for to say;
The damage has been done, it's proved,
They'll have to go away.'

Oh, bloody hell and balderdash,
My teeth will hang on hooks!
They'll grate and grind and spit and splash,
And spoil my bloody looks!

The first set weren't as desired,
I fumed and cursed a lot;
My consternation was all fired -
What choice was it I'd got?

And then a friendly Scot stepped in
And showed me where to go;
Said the denture man, 'Oh, it's a sin -
Let's show you what I know!'

The denture man was such a star -
He did it all for cash -
He said, 'You're fixed, you really are,
Or my name isn't Nash!'

He dug above and underneath,
And round about my tongue;
His brand new set of 'gnashing' teeth
Have made me feel so young.

I've regained all my former style,
I'm feeling fine and dandy;
I'll give a glowing, grateful smile -
To my faithful, good friend, Sandy.

Sandy Splitt

THE SAD TALE OF ETHEL WHO ATE FAR TOO MUCH!

As Ethel gobbled up her crisps
She noticed growth upon her hips
And as she stuffed her face with Brie
She spotted bulges on her knee
As pastry accessed Ethel's jaws
She witnessed growing rearside flaws
And *still* she ate another chop
And seven rolls - she couldn't stop
The ten jam tarts she'd made for tea
Were finished off with splendid glee
Her pre-cooked dinners for the week
Were swiftly stuffed into her cheek
And even as her gullet jammed
She could not quite resist the ham
Her body stretched at quite a rate
To safely buffer chips and skate
But then her gullet could take no more
A queue of food stuck in her craw
Her folds of fat fell to the floor
And then her tum let out a roar
And rent - you've never seen the like
Her spleen flew out like a lightning strike
Her gastrointestinal wall
Burst with gusto in the hall
And Ethel fell upon the ground
Wailing like a basset hound . . .
But even as she gasped her last
Her greedy little fingers clasped
A straying crumb from 'neath her head
And this she ate. Then fell down dead.

Anon

PLEASURE?
(With acknowledgement to W H Davies)

What is this life if, full of cares,
We are concerned with stocks and shares?

We have no time to stand about,
We must jump up and down and shout.

How low the Footsie is today!
We may not get our normal pay.

It could even mean that we'll go broke
And have to work like normal folk.

No bonus of a million pounds,
No drinks at five hundred quid a round.

We could even go from riches to rags,
Oh why did we decide to become stags?

A poor life this for us we feel,
But there might be time for one more deal.

Bill Fletcher

THE FUN NEVER STOPS WITH JUNK!

When old Mrs Nifferty opened the post,
Her heart filled with joy, a house on the coast,
To be hers for a fortnight, in June every year,
Instead of her shack on the edge of the square.
She filled in the coupon, the tie-breaker too,
She felt so elated, she went to the zoo,
Her passion, the snake house, the spiders and bats,
The owls and the monkeys and last the big cats!
Back home with her feet up, she looked through the mail,
A cruise on a liner, which day will it sail?
She filled in the coupon, to find out which day
She could set out for Melbourne or Botany Bay!
New sofa, new covers, new windows, new door,
On offer at half price, what could she do more?
She filled in the coupon, she would hear in a week,
So she ordered a new roof, it might stop the leak!
Her paintwork looked shabby, on offer, guess what?
Textured wall coating that cures damp and rot!
She filled in the coupon and longed for her dream
To start coming true, so she ate strawberries and cream!
Money on offer, she could borrow it all,
Heat her home, have a cooker and have a real ball!
The booking form posted, her phone grew quite hot,
They all wanted money, some a little, some a lot!
She looked at her pension, her savings and thought,
The fun never stops, but it gets a bit fraught!
So old Mrs Nifferty, with problems and pain,
Bought a flat with her sister, in warm sunny Spain!
She sold her damp house to a lady from Crewe,
Who opened a café and called it Boy Blue!

Norma Rudge

NAUGHTY NATASHA

There was a young, opinionated chatterbox called Natasha,
Who went to school dressed only in her stripy pyjamas!
Despite high intelligence, being indolent and silly,
On a cold winter's day, it was so chilly,
She came back home blue and frozen in a block of ice,
No incessant chatter nor inquisitive natter, how blissful. how quiet,

how nice!

Robin Halder

A WOMAN'S LOT

We wear them each and every day
to hoist, control and separate,
with straps and bones and underwires . . .
those weird contraptions that we hate!
Though they can help, we still bemoan
a woman's lot of wobble and bounce,
and as I know cows don't wear bras
I'm asking this, 'Why then should we?'

Jennifer Richards

A PRESENT DAY HELEN OF TROY

If your face is your fortune as they say,
I think I ran out of cash today.
The crows have worked out with their big feet,
Over my laugh lines, which were small and neat.
My lips are crinkly, my jaws are saggy,
Oh dear my neck is getting baggy!
I've stayed out the sun, I gave up the fags,
I followed the advice in all the mags.
But my face is really a map of my life,
Full of love and laughter, tears and strife.
I think Botox and facelifts are so uncool,
I won't be having them at all.
Besides I don't think grandmas oughta
End up looking like their daughter's daughter!

Judy Hopkin

THE FLOWER ARRANGER PREPARES

See the flower arranger gathering her wares.
Containers fill the table top, material drapes the chairs.
Foliage fills the buckets lined up in the hall.
Moss is wrapped in paper in a big untidy ball.
There's wire and there's oasis, secateurs and string,
Ribbons, clips and holders and rolls of foil and 'cling'.
Flowers stand in bunches, driftwood's stacked in piles . . .
As she surveys the chaos the flower arranger smiles.
She's filled with great excitement as she's about to start
Her own interpretation of the floral artist's art.
Meanwhile, her poor husband, who's been waiting for his 'grub',
Has decided to abandon ship and set off to the pub!

Peter Doole

I DO STILL LOVE YOU DARLING

I do still love you darling despite what everyone thinks
Although you bring me bad luck like a chain without no links
I met you at the bus stop just you and me alone
The bus broke down just after and I had to walk back home
I took you for a meal I thought that couldn't fail
Then someone stole my chequebook and I spent the night in jail
That night you cooked a meal for me when I first went to your home
I spent the night in hospital after swallowing a big fish bone
Then at our engagement we had problems with the mains
The disco caught on fire and the place went up in flames
Even at our wedding things did not go to plan
When your mother the man-eater went off with my best man
We were waiting in the church; the candles had burned to ash
With no sign of the vicar, he was in a bad car crash
Then we bought our first home, an old building you had found
But then when all the storms came it was blown down to the ground
That day you came to work with me, the bottles I asked you to stack
You smashed five hundred of them and I then got the sack
Even in our old age things still go wrong the same
You've cost me literally thousands but I battle against the strain
I do still love you darling despite what everyone thinks
I know you bring me bad luck; you're nothing but a jinx

Kram

FALSTAFF

Falstaff, he was a noble knight
Sir John his title little worth
Not acclaimed for prowess in a fight
His fame lay rather in his mighty girth.

Eastcheap in London was his patch
Much ale he quaffed, its colour pale
The gallons flowed. That was the catch,
Drink was Sir John's Holy Grail.

Gadshill, Bardolph, Peto, Poins
Boon companions all, were pledged to drink
Falstaff, their leader, girds his lions
Drink, among them, was the common link.

The gallant knight no good in fight
Would strike a blow or two then run.
More of a bounder was he prone to flight
Never to join battle when set upon.

Prince Hal was a loving mate
Later to become England's king.
Falstaff was no minister of state
The waspish clown had curbed his sting.

Angus Richmond

TRAFFIC LIGHTS

The traffic lights outside the supermarket
Have a very strange effect
On my friend Margaret
On our return from eating out at lunch
The red light glows
And we halt with a crunch

We sit there so engrossed
In the previous day's deeds
The lights go to green, then red
Then once more to green

What can we be thinking of
Glued there at the lights
Is it temporary insanity
No -
I think we're all right

That fellow just behind us
In the fast red car
Is a tiny bit irate
But -
We also have a hunch -

He'll forgive us
If we smile at him
And maybe next week
Take us out to lunch.

Pat Plant

OUR HEROES IN TIGHTS

We rush to our screens to see our heroes in tights,
Our cape crusaders are taking flight!
'It looks like another Penguin fight.'
Our saviours from the Gotham City night,
They flee past the buildings giving us delight!
They are so brave and cool in their capes,
As they swing through the heavy window drapes;
The fight starts and Robin hits out 'pow'
'Boom'. 'Holy mackerel,' Robin screams!
'Batman help me now!'

Batman comes as cool as can be,
Fighting hard to help Robin to be free,
They fight together banging heads on the way,
It's comical to watch - the henchmen falling away.
The Penguin flees through the window into the night,
Giving the public on the sidewalk a terrible fright!

The Batmobile is waiting for the crusaders to get in,
To speed off to the Batcave, and put their costumes in the bin.
They move back into society as if nothing has happened at all,
Waiting for the red bat phone to go again, and answer another call . . .

Ricky N Lock

SUBMISSIONS INVITED
SOMETHING FOR EVERYONE

POETRY NOW 2004 - Any subject,
any style, any time.

WOMENSWORDS 2004 - Strictly women,
have your say the female way!

STRONGWORDS 2004 - Warning!
Opinionated and have strong views.
(Not for the faint-hearted)

All poems no longer than 30 lines.
Always welcome! No fee!
Cash Prizes to be won!

Mark your envelope (eg *Poetry Now*) *2004*
Send to:
Forward Press Ltd
Remus House, Coltsfoot Drive,
Peterborough, PE2 9JX

OVER £10,000 POETRY PRIZES
TO BE WON!

Judging will take place in October 2004